GLIMPSES OF ETERNITY

An Investigation into Shared Death Experiences

RAYMOND MOODY Jr., M.D., Ph.D.

WITH PAUL PERRY

RIDER

LONDON · SYDNEY · AUCKLAND · JOHANNESBURG

1 3 5 7 9 10 8 6 4 2

Published in 2010 by Rider, an imprint of Ebury Publishing
First published in the USA by Guideposts in 2010

Ebury Publishing is a Random House Group company

Copyright © Raymond Moody with Paul Perry, 2010

Raymond Moody with Paul Perry have asserted their right to be identified as the
authors of this work in accordance with the Copyright, Designs and Patents Act 1988.

The Random House Group Limited Reg. No. 954009

Addresses for companies within the Random House Group can be found at
www.rbooks.co.uk

A CIP catalogue record for this book is available from the British Library

The Random House Group Limited supports The Forest Stewardship
Council (FSC), the leading international forest certification organisation.
All our titles that are printed on Greenpeace approved FSC certified paper carry the
FSC logo. Our paper procurement policy can be found at
www.rbooks.co.uk/environment

Mixed Sources
Product group from well-managed
forests and other controlled sources
www.fsc.org Cert no. TT-COC-2139
© 1996 Forest Stewardship Council

Printed and bound in Great Britain by CPI Mackays, Chatham ME5 8TD

ISBN 9781846042539

Copies are available at special rates for bulk orders. Contact the sales development
team on 020 7840 8487 for more information.

To buy books by your favourite authors and register for offers, visit
www.rbooks.co.uk

To my children and grandchild.
—Raymond Moody

To Paige, my daughter and friend.
—Paul Perry

And to our agent Nat Sobel, who has provided guidance for three decades. With great appreciation, love and friendship.
—Raymond and Paul

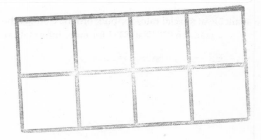

CONTENTS

"Accident is the name of the greatest of all inventors."

—MARK TWAIN

I

AN ACCIDENTAL DISCOVERY

BY THE TIME I ARRIVED at medical school in 1972, I was already famous for the research I had done into what I called the near-death experience. Although I had not yet written about these experiences, I had spoken publicly so many times about my findings that I was well-known even as a first-year student.

I didn't "invent death," as some people have jokingly said to me. What I did do was examine the experiences of several people who had almost died, breaking down the process of dying into its identifiable elements. Collectively, I called the combination of all or several of those traits the "near-death experience."

What I found amazed me, and later when I collected my findings into the book *Life After Life*, it amazed the world. I discovered that it was common for the dying to pass through a tunnel on their way to a light. In this light they would often meet other spiritual beings that were there to ease their transition into death. Many times these spiritual beings were deceased relatives. Sometimes they were beings that the subjects described as "God" or "Jesus." It was not uncommon for the subjects to tell of conversations with Jesus, or to be told by God that it wasn't their time to die.

Many of the subjects recounted leaving their bodies and watching from above as doctors and nurses took heroic measures to save their lives. A lot of the people I spoke with had life reviews, in which they "lived" their lives again, sometimes with commentary from a higher being.

Rarely did these people want to return to their physical bodies, but when they did they had a profound sense of higher purpose—a belief that there is some further duty to be done on earth before leaving for a spiritual realm.

These were experiences and accounts not yet found in medical books, and because of that, there were those who expected my research and the subsequent book to be real trouble for me. As a medical student researching something that could be construed as spiritual or even religious, I was opening myself to the prejudices that the world of science is thought to have about such matters. Even though the elements of the near-death experience had hidden in plain view since man first pondered death, their exploration was a form of heresy that would ostracize me from the scientific community.

That is what some of my close friends thought.

Personally, I was less concerned about acceptance by the medical school staff than my friends were. Like most people throughout history, including doctors, I had heard and read of "supernatural" events taking place at the moment of death. These were familiar to me through both my reading and my own life experience. As a student and teacher of philosophy, I had read many such accounts of the afterlife, including those recorded in the works of Plato. And then there are those accounts of our spiritual body in the Bible, particularly Saint Paul's letter to the Corinthians, in which he writes: "There is a natural body, and there is a spiritual body...Behold, I show you a mystery: We shall not all sleep, but we shall all be changed."

Great literature, too, deals with elements of near-death experiences. Scrooge's uncomfortable life review in Charles Dickens's *A Christmas Carol* is one such example, and Ernest Hemingway's out-of-body experience during combat in *For Whom the Bell Tolls* is another.

Then, there are stories we hear from friends and family. For me there was my cousin Ronnie, who nearly died after surgery. He spoke of entering a heavenly realm, where he was told by a being of light that he would not return to his physical body if he crossed a particular boundary. Ronnie said he turned and ran as hard as he could, all the way back to his body. And then there was the story told by George Ritchie, a doctor in Charlottesville, Virginia, who had been declared dead at a military hospital in Texas only to have one of the most amazing near-death experiences ever—one that included an out-of-body journey that took him across the country and that was so vivid he was later able to follow the route after he recovered. It was truly Ritchie's story that led me to collect similar experiences from students in my philosophy classes at East Carolina University, where I was teaching, and to search these for the common elements that together became known as the "near-death experience."

When word got out that I was studying this phenomenon, people who had almost died contacted me in every way possible. Through my research they realized that their experience was not unique, but was one that had happened, in some form or other, to millions of people worldwide. My doorbell rang almost as often as my telephone with people who wanted to tell their stories and receive confirmation that they were not insane or delusional. They were as relieved to discover that others had had similar experiences as I was to gain another case study. When a person approached me in public and whispered, "I have a story you won't believe..." my heart would begin to race with excitement. I still have the same reaction all these decades later. And yes, many of these case studies have come from doctors.

Near-death studies warmly received

It came as no surprise to me that when I started medical school at the age of twenty-four, I was generously received by the teaching staff of the Medical College of Georgia. Within two weeks of starting classes, no fewer than eight professors invited me to their offices or their homes to discuss near-death experiences.

One of these was Dr. Claude Starr-Wright, a hematology professor who found himself in the unenviable position of having to resuscitate a friend whose heart had stopped. To Claude's great surprise, the patient became quite angry after being brought back from the brink of death. When Claude inquired further, he discovered that his friend had had a near-death experience that took him to a place so heavenly he did not want to return.

Other physicians told me about their own startling experiences with death, all of which contained puzzling elements that they couldn't put into words until they heard about my research and understood that what they had witnessed was a near-death experience.

I heard many stories during those first few months of medical school, all of which fit neatly into the description of a near-death experience as defined in my work. It seemed as though every week or so I would hear another story from a doctor, nurse or patient that involved a mysterious account of the afterlife. It was thrilling to have this steady stream of material that validated the findings of my research.

Then something happened to change all of that.

I was standing at the school's magazine stand reading an article about Gorgeous George, a well-known wrestler from the 1950s, when an attractive woman approached me and held out her hand.

"Raymond, I'm Dr. Jamieson," she said, shaking my hand.

She was a respected member of the faculty, so much so that I was somewhat embarrassed to be reading an article about a wrestler in a men's magazine. I tried to conceal the magazine, but the fact of the matter was that Dr. Jamieson didn't care. Her mother had died recently, she said, and something had happened during her death that she had not seen in my research nor heard of from anyone else.

With a pleasant insistence, she asked if I could accompany her to her office so she could tell me in private what had happened. When we were comfortably ensconced, she told me a story the likes of which I had never before heard.

"To begin with, let me tell you that I was not raised in a religious family," she said. "That doesn't mean my parents were against religion—they just didn't have an opinion about it. As a result, I never thought about the afterlife because it was not a subject that came up in our household.

"Anyway, about two years ago, my mother had a cardiac arrest. It was unexpected and happened at home. I happened to be visiting her when it took place and had to work on her with CPR. Can you imagine what it's like to give your mother mouth-to-mouth resuscitation? It is difficult enough on a stranger, but it was almost inconceivable to do it on my *own* mother.

"I continued to work on her for a long time, maybe thirty minutes or so, until I realized that any further effort was futile and that she was dead. At that point I stopped and caught my breath. I was exhausted and I can honestly say that it hadn't yet sunk in that I was now an orphan."

Suddenly, Dr. Jamieson felt herself lift out of her body. She realized that she was above her own body and the now-deceased body of her mother, looking down on the whole scene as though she were on a balcony.

"Being out-of-body took me aback," she said. "As I was trying to get my bearings I suddenly became aware that my mother was now hovering with me in spirit form. She was right next to me!"

Dr. Jamieson calmly said good-bye to her mother, who was now smiling and quite happy, a stark contrast to her corpse down below. Then Dr. Jamieson saw something else that surprised her.

"I looked in the corner of the room and became aware of a breach in the universe that was pouring light like water coming from a broken pipe. Out of that light came people I had known for years, deceased friends of my mother. But there were other people there as well, people I didn't recognize but I assume they were friends of my mother's whom I didn't know."

As Dr. Jamieson watched, her mother drifted off into the light. The last Dr. Jamieson saw of her mother, she said, was her having a very tender reunion with all of her friends. "Then the tube closed down in an almost spiral fashion, like a camera lens, and the light was gone," she said.

How long this all lasted Dr. Jamieson didn't know. But when it ended she found herself back in her body, standing next to her deceased mother, totally puzzled about what had just happened.

"What do you make of that story?" she asked.

I could only shrug. At this point I had heard dozens of regular near-death experiences, and was hearing new ones each week. But there was little about Dr. Jamieson's experience that I could comment on, since this was the first of this kind I had ever encountered.

"I said, what do you make of the story?" she asked again.

"It's empathic," I said, using the word that means the ability to share another's feelings. "It is a shared death experience."

"Have you heard many of these?" she asked, clearly excited at the notion that I had.

"No, Dr. Jamieson, I haven't," I said. "I am afraid that yours is the first I have ever heard."

Dr. Jamieson and I sat in her office, making small talk about the nature of the experience she'd had with her mother. But in the end, we were completely puzzled, unable to figure out what had happened.

Shared death experience . . . The phrase stuck in my mind, but I didn't hear another until the mid-1980s, when I began to hear stories from nurses and doctors about curious events that took place at deathbeds. Attitudes in medicine had loosened up by then. I began to realize that shared death experiences have been with us since the beginning of medicine; it's just that doctors and nurses have been discouraged from speaking about events that could be considered more spiritual than scientific. As one doctor from the "olden days" told me, "It was almost treated as a violation of our oath as physicians to talk about anything that could be considered spiritual in nature. You just let it go—you didn't talk about it."

But that was then. By the 1980s, they were opening up, talking about all kinds of things, including near-death experiences and shared death experiences.

After I finished medical school, I began bringing up stories of empathic or shared death experiences at medical conferences all around the world. Sometimes I heard stories from people who were on the medical frontlines and were ready to talk, and gradually it became obvious to me that these experiences happened more frequently than I had thought. It also became obvious that they had common ground with near-death experiences, although I have to say there were many traits that I'd never heard of.

For instance, I began to hear people talking about the room changing shape and a mystical light that filled the room—both things I had never heard of with near-death experiences. But of all the recurring elements in these shared death experiences, among the most startling was the joint review of a loved one's life.

A woman I'll call Susan told me the sad but remarkable story of her adult son's death from cancer. I think it's remarkable because of the information she received. As the man died, she was "swept up in a cloud" with him and witnessed many scenes from his life. Some of the scenes were familiar to her, such as those from his childhood and teenage years. Others were completely alien to her, like those from what she called "his private years." She wouldn't elaborate on what those scenes may have held, other than to say, "I wasn't embarrassed in the least by anything I saw."

The information this woman gathered from her son's life review was so specific that when it was over, she was able to recognize his friends and visit places that she had seen in the shared vision.

I was struck by this woman's shared death experience because she received information that was previously unknown to her and which proved to be correct when checked out. She was not revisiting her own memories. But I still didn't know what to make of such case studies, other than to acknowledge that, in each experience, a doorway seemed to open to a new aspect of the person who had died.

"Everything we did was there in that light"

Here is another such story, told in its entirety by Dana, a woman whose shared life review with her husband was vivid and contained images and events that she had previously been unaware of. Here is her entire story in her own words:

"It was on my husband Johnny's fifty-fifth birthday when the doctor told us that Johnny had lung cancer and had maybe about six months to live. I felt like somebody had hit me with a baseball bat. Honestly, I don't even remember the doctor saying the words; it was like I just gradually figured out what he was saying.

"The next day I just walked into the bank and quit my job then and there. From that day until Johnny died, we weren't separated from each other more than a few hours. I was beside him the whole time in the hospital and was holding onto him when he died. When he did, he went right through my body. It felt like an electric sensation, like when you get your finger in the electrical socket, only much more gentle.

"Anyway, when that happened our whole life sprang up around us and just kind of swallowed up the hospital room and everything in it in an instant. There was light all around: a bright, white light that I immediately knew—and Johnny knew—was Christ.

"Everything we ever did was there in that light. Plus I saw things about Johnny . . . I saw him doing things before we were married. You might think that some of it might be embarrassing or personal, and it was. But there was no need for privacy, as strange as that might seem. These were things that Johnny did before we were married. Still, I saw him with girls when he was very young. Later I searched for them in his high school yearbook and was able to find them, just based on what I saw during the life review during his death.

"In the middle of this life review, I saw myself there holding onto his dead body, which didn't make me feel bad because he was also completely alive, right beside me, viewing our life together.

"By the way, the life review was like a 'wraparound.' I don't know how else to describe it. It was a wraparound scene of everything Johnny and I experienced together or apart. There is no way I could even put it into words other than to say that all of this was in a flash, right there at the bedside where my husband died.

"Then, right in the middle of this review, the child that we lost to a miscarriage when I was still a teenager stepped forth and embraced us. She was not a figure of a person exactly as you would see a human being, but more the outline or sweet, loving presence of a little girl. The upshot of her being there was that any issues we ever had regarding her loss were made whole and resolved. I was reminded of the verse from the Bible about 'the peace that passeth all understanding.' That's how I felt when she was there.

"One of the funny things about this wraparound view of our life was that we had gone to Atlanta in the seventh grade, to the state capitol, where there was a diorama. So at one point we were watching this wraparound and watching ourselves in another wraparound—a diorama—where we stood side by side as kids. I burst out laughing and Johnny laughed too, right there beside me.

"Another thing that was strange about this wraparound was that in certain parts of it there were panels or dividers that kept us from seeing all of it. I don't have the words for this, but these screens or panels kept particular parts of both of our lives invisible. I don't know what was behind them but I do know that these were thoughts from Christ, who said that someday we would be able to see behind those panels too."

"A bright light appeared in the room"

Other versions of shared death experiences that baffled me were those events that were shared by several people at the bedside. It is possible for a skeptic to easily write off a dying person's death experience when it is shared with only one other person. But a death experience shared with a number of people at the bedside is more difficult to pass off as an individual fantasy.

Take, for example, the experience of the Anderson family, from a suburb of Atlanta, as they sat by their dying mother. This is told by one of the sisters, but all who were there corroborate the account:

"The day my mother died, my two brothers, my sister, my sister–in–law and I were all in the room. My mother hadn't spoken a word in several hours, and she was breathing in an irregular pattern. None of us were really upset because mother had been on a long downhill course and we knew this was the end.

"Suddenly, a bright light appeared in the room. My first thought was that a reflection was shining through the window from a vehicle passing by outside. Even as I thought that, however, I knew it wasn't true, because this was not any kind of light on this earth. I nudged my sister to see if she saw it too, and when I looked at her, her eyes were as big as saucers. At the same time I saw my brother literally gasp. Everyone saw it together and for a little while we were frightened.

"Then my mother just expired and we all kind of breathed a big sigh of relief. At that moment, we saw vivid bright lights that seemed to gather around and shape up into . . . I don't know what to call it except an entranceway. The lights looked a bit like clouds, but that is only a comparison. We saw my mother lift

*up out of her body and go through that entranceway. Being by
the entranceway, incidentally, was a feeling of complete joy. My
brother called it a chorus of joyful feelings, and my sister heard
beautiful music, although none of the rest of us did.*

*"I am originally from Virginia and my sister, brother and
I agreed that the entranceway was shaped something like the
Natural Bridge in the Shenandoah Valley. The lights were so
vivid we had no choice but to tell our story to the hospice nurse.*

*"She listened and then told us that she knew of similar
things happening and that it was not uncommon for the dying
process to encompass people nearby."*

Another case that serves to illustrate the sharing of a
death experience by more than one person comes from
two women in their forties who were the first to tell me
about jointly sharing the life review of a dying loved one.
I'll call them Pat and Nancy.

The sisters were at their mother's bedside as she was
dying of lung cancer. As her breathing became more labored, the room began to "light up," said one of the sisters.
Both of them told of how the room began to swirl, quickly
at first before slowing to a stop. Then the two women
found themselves standing with their mother, who looked
decades younger.

Together, they were immersed in their mother's life
review, which was filled with many scenes they had
lived and many they had not. They saw their mother's
first boyfriend and experienced her heartbreak at their
breakup. They saw small things that had meant a lot to
their mother, like the times she had helped poor children

at their school without telling anyone. They also discovered the feelings their mother had for a widower who lived down the street, and how she had longed to strike up a conversation with him.

"What we saw was so real that we thought we had died too," said one of the sisters. "For months it was beyond belief until we finally accepted it."

Seeing the unknown

Perhaps the most peculiar of all shared death experiences that I heard in the early days are the ones I called "predictive experiences," in which the shared death experience reveals the death of someone else who is not expected to die anytime soon. These experiences truly puzzled me when I first heard them, and still do to this day.

Below is a predictive shared death experience that was told to me by Daniel, a hospice worker in Greenville, North Carolina:

"An elderly man with Alzheimer's disease was the first patient of mine who fits the description you offered of an empathic near-death experience. Mr. Sykes, the man with Alzheimer's, declined quite rapidly for his illness and age and died about a year after diagnosis. I got to know him and his wife quite well during our time together.

"About two months before his death he lapsed into what I would call an almost vegetative state. It was a typical last stage of Alzheimer's disease. He didn't know where he was nor did

*he recognize his wife or children. He could not talk coherently
and gave no sign of understanding anything about his circumstances. The week before he died the nurse and I saw him twitch
violently.*

*"The day he died was different in a very eerie way. He sat up
in bed and spoke as clear as a bell, talking just like anyone would,
but not addressing us. He was looking upward with bright eyes
and carrying on a conversation with 'Hugh.' He spoke loud and
clear to Hugh, sometimes laughing but usually just convers-
ing as though the two were sitting in a coffee shop having a
chat."*

The hospice workers assumed that Hugh was a deceased relative, but Mr. Sykes's wife cleared up that mis-
perception, telling them that he was her husband's brother
and lived in Massachusetts. She had just spoken to him a
day or so earlier, she said, to tell him that her husband was
on his deathbed.

*"Mr. Sykes's wife told us that Hugh was alive and in good
health, but of course, as you can guess, we learned shortly afterward that Hugh had keeled over with a fatal heart attack
right about the time that Mr. Sykes miraculously came back to
life."*

When Mrs. Sykes found out that Hugh had died suddenly, her husband's conversation with him took on another dimension for everyone at the bedside, said the
hospice worker. They had initially believed that Mr. Sykes
was in the throes of dementia. Now they saw him as being

in communication with his newly deceased brother while he lay on his own deathbed.

Artifacts of observation

By the late 1990s, I was hearing stories of shared death experiences from all over the world. Although I was able to collect many such stories, I did not have enough to draw any conclusions from them. Because of that, I had come to regard them as medical artifacts—unexpected findings that can be researched later and may lead to important conclusions.

The history of medicine is filled with artifacts that have later been explored and have changed the way patients are treated or viewed. For example, Barry J. Marshall and J. Robin Warren, physicians from Perth, Australia, noticed that patients who were on antibiotics for other reasons would also experience a healing of their stomach ulcers. They published a study showing that many stomach ulcers are caused by a bacterium and not stress, as most experts had believed.

Although these doctors were ridiculed when they presented their findings at a number of conferences of gastroenterologists, some of the doctors present conducted their own studies and found that the Australian doctors were right. Their findings—based on their own observations—changed the way many stomach ulcers are treated. This breakthrough—and their perseverance in the belief that it was important—won the two doctors the 2005

Nobel Prize in Physiology or Medicine for "the discovery of the bacterium *Helicobacter pylori* and its role in gastritis and peptic ulcers."

There are many such examples of artifacts in medicine, subject areas that hint at future lines of research. For the time being, that was what I considered shared death experiences to be. I knew they existed. I knew they held fascinating information that could affect the future of near-death studies. I just didn't have enough case studies from which to draw any real conclusions, only questions about what little I knew about those experiences. I had to wait for more stories to come in. I had to be patient.

"Dying is something we human beings do continuously, not just at the end of our physical lives on this earth."

—DR. ELISABETH KÜBLER-ROSS

2

FLOOD OF STORIES

BEFORE THE GROUNDBREAKING WORK of Dr. Elisabeth Kübler-Ross, the terminally ill were largely left to die alone. Back in the 1970s, few family members were allowed at the bedside of a dying patient. In those days, it was believed that death was something only trained medical professionals could handle. Instead of allowing family members to gather at the hospital bedside of a dying loved one, doctors and nurses would tenderly escort the family members out to a waiting room. This paternalistic act was inspired by the belief that watching a loved one die was too traumatic. Rather, it was the duty of the doctors and nurses—veterans at death—to absorb the pain and suffering.

Thanks to the work of Dr. Elisabeth Kübler-Ross and the subsequent rise of the hospice movement, medical attitudes toward death and dying have changed considerably. Now, doctors and nurses encourage family members to be at the bedside of a dying loved one, even taking over management of the deathbed scene if they feel comfortable doing so.

The New York Times, in its 2004 obituary of Kübler-Ross, summed up how the medical system dealt with death before her 1969 bestseller *Death and Dying*: "Terminally ill patients were routinely left to face death in a miasma of loneliness and fear, because doctors, nurses and families were generally ill equipped to deal with death."

The work of Kübler-Ross helped end the taboos in many Western cultures against openly discussing and studying death. It also helped change the care of terminally ill patients to make death less psychologically painful, not only for the dying but also for their doctors and nurses—and for the survivors. Perhaps nothing sums up the work of Kübler-Ross better than a comment she once made to me: "I always say that death can be one of the greatest experiences ever," she said. "We realize now that we don't have to cure to heal. We need only provide pain relief, kindness and friendship. Dying is as natural as birth."

Kübler-Ross's book was published around the time I began my own studies into near-death experiences. Even in 1972—three years after the publication of her book—the subject of death was still in its taboo phase. But it began to thaw quickly as our individual work gave the medical profession freedom to discuss the clinical and spiritual aspects of death.

As I have already mentioned, I was researching the case studies that would become the basis for my work on near-death experiences when I began medical school. In 1975, a small Georgia publisher, Mockingbird Press, published my first book, *Life After Life*. In the foreword, Kübler-Ross wrote: "We have learned a lot about the process of dying, but we still have many questions with regard to the moment of death and to the experience our patients have when they are pronounced medically dead. It is research such as Dr. Moody presents in his book that will enlighten many and will confirm what we have been taught for two thousand years—that there is life after death."

I appreciated Elisabeth's belief that I had proven life after death and that I would enlighten many with my work on the process of death. My publisher, John Egle, appreciated her kind words as well. He fervently believed, much to my pride and joy, that our little book might sell as many as five thousand copies.

So it became a shock to both of us when "many" turned out to be millions! *Life After Life* rapidly became a huge best seller and eventually one of the best-selling nonfiction books of all time, a publishing phenomenon that revealed a yearning for information about what happens when we die.

Of course I was pleased that I had written an international best seller. But the greatest blessing of *Life After Life* for me was the entrée it gave me into people's deepest thoughts about mankind's oldest question: What happens when we die? As a result of writing the book,

I was granted the freedom to ask people most any question about death, and the honor of receiving honest, well-thought-out answers as well as more questions.

Letters and stories came in constantly from those who'd had near-death experiences as well as those who knew people who had. Mail came in large bags from the post office, and the phone rang constantly. It was as though a dam holding back a flood of common experiences had broken and suddenly they were washing over my world. And those experiences came from people in every walk of life, including medicine.

As anyone who has dealt with doctors knows, they can be a skeptical bunch. It makes sense: I really don't think that most patients would like the results of their treatment if they dealt with doctors who didn't demand proof every step of the way. The fact that most doctors base their medical care on research-based evidence is good for the patient as well as the profession. Yet despite their reputation for skepticism, hundreds of people who work in medicine sent me stories of near-death experiences. It seemed as though doctors, like everyone else, needed to vent their experiences with death and dying. They found near-death studies to be a brand-new field into which they could contribute their heretofore-private stories.

Whether I was on a book tour or speaking at medical conferences, I was constantly approached by doctors and nurses who told me touching stories about near-death experiences and other spiritual events that had taken place during the latter moments of their patients' lives.

Many of the stories they told me involved shared death experiences.

A change of perspective

At a medical conference in Kentucky, a tall, pleasant physician expressed gratitude to me for founding the field of near-death studies. It had changed many things for him, both personally and professionally, he said. He then proceeded to tell me a story about the death of his mother, which took place after a bout with cancer that lasted nearly a year.

According to this doctor—I will call him Tom—he was fully prepared for his mother's death. The two had openly discussed her imminent passing, largely so the death itself would not be so wrenchingly emotional.

Up until that point, the thought of life after death had not entered the picture. Tom had not been raised to believe in the concept, and since his mother did the raising, she did not believe in it either. And although he had read about the growing field of near-death studies, Tom felt that the unusual pre-death happenings were merely dreamlike experiences created by the dying brain. In short, Tom was not raised to believe what would happen at his mother's bedside.

"I was standing at the foot of her bed watching her as she struggled for breath," said Tom. "The head of the bed was elevated so the effect was almost as though she was sitting up looking at me, only she wasn't, because her eyes were closed and she was well within herself at this time."

The next thing Tom knew, the room began to change shape ever so slightly and the light—which had been subdued—became very bright and gave Tom a sense that it had substance to it. "I was frightened," he said. "I thought I was having a stroke or some other neurological problem."

Tom noticed that his mother was responding to the light too, but not in a way he had ever seen. She "sat up," but not physically. Rather, "I saw this film or transparent envelope of light close up and lift off her body going upwards and out of sight," he said.

It was immediately apparent to Tom that his mother had died and the light was her spirit leaving her physical body.

"It happened in just a moment," said Tom. "But it turned the shock I felt at my mother's death into great joyousness at her manner of departure. I do not remember ever having seriously thought about life after death before that moment. But when I saw her leave her body it became an instant realization that she went to another place. What would have been deep grief turned immediately to great joy!"

Although Tom had never told anyone except his wife about what happened, he began to freely discuss the mystery of death and other spiritual experiences with his patients and their families. Now, when he hears a patient say, "You won't believe what happened to me when I had my heart attack," he sits down with the person and listens as they share the wonderment of what happened to them.

"One thing I want to make sure is that people who have these experiences don't feel crazy," said Tom. "But I never tell them what happened to me when my mom died. I feel as though I have to keep that to myself."

Tom was relieved to find that I'd heard other such stories, enough of them, in fact, that I had developed a name—shared death experiences—for them. But when he asked if I knew what they meant, I could only shrug. "I'm in the process of collecting these stories now," I said.

Lucky to see the mist

A similar story came to me from a nurse named Millie Davis who began working in the newly formed field of hospice care after the event she related to me. She was at the bedside of her dying father along with her mother and sister. Her father was in the end stages of lung cancer and had been in a coma for an entire day. The three most important women in his life had gathered in the hospital room before he went into the coma, and all three were now exhausted.

Millie was sleeping on a small couch facing her father, while her sister and mother were slumped uncomfortably in a pair of Naugahyde chairs that had been brought into the room by the hospital staff. The three were sleeping in fits and starts, waking up to noises from other parts of the hospital or finding themselves stirred by the unsteady breathing of the dying man.

At about 2:00 AM, Millie awoke and listened to her father's breathing. He had a death rattle by now, and she knew he would not be alive much longer. She asked herself: *Should I wake up my mom and sister? Should I wait until he dies? What if he doesn't die soon? They are both so exhausted and need their sleep.* Then Millie sat up to take a closer look at her father. Two pillars of light stood next to the bed.

"They looked just like pillars of light but I am sure they were guardian angels," said Millie. "There was something about them that put me at ease and made me think they had come to comfort him."

Millie stood up. Her father's breathing had become erratic now and she knew he was about to die. As she approached the bed, she noticed a mist arise from his chest, as if off a still river. It hovered over him for a few seconds and then dissipated, which surprised Millie.

"I always thought that if I saw something like a soul leave the body it would zoom straight up. But this just sat there like fog and then went away," she said. "I was very surprised."

After having this shared death experience with her father, Millie switched specialties and became a hospice nurse. She told me that she has seen the mist rising from many patients as they die. "Other nurses see even more, including the patient get up from his dying body and walk away," she said. "I feel lucky enough just to see the mist. But, Dr. Moody, what does it mean and how does it happen?"

"What do you make of that?"

Another member of the medical profession asked me the same thing. Ted was a physician's assistant and paramedic who worked at a hospital in the Deep South. One day the paramedics got a call to go to an address near the hospital where a man was reported to have attempted suicide.

When Ted and the other medics rushed into the house, they realized to their horror that the man who had attempted suicide was a psychologist at the hospital. Ted was well acquainted with the man and knew that his wife had recently left him. He had witnessed a sea change in how the doctor related to others. He had been talkative and friendly, but in recent months he had become withdrawn and somber.

And now this.

Ted knelt over the man and realized that he was dead. Still, he began to administer CPR, more out of instinct than out of hope. His attempts were to no avail, and within about ten minutes he gave up.

That was when he became aware of the man standing next to him. It was the psychologist in spirit form, and he was looking down at his own body with a look of amazement and regret on his face.

As far as Ted knows, none of the other medics saw the spirit being. As he stared up at the dead man's spirit, he had the sense that the man was curious about what would happen next.

And what happened wasn't pleasant.

The next-door neighbor had seen the ambulance and came over to see what was going on. When he saw that the psychologist was dead, he made a cutting remark. Ted doesn't remember what the man said, but he did recall the spirit's reaction. He said the spirit seemed to shrink, as though he was shriveling from the hurt caused by the comment.

"It was painful for me to watch," said Ted. "It was as though the life was sucked out of him, like he had been drained by what the neighbor said."

Ted didn't see the spirit after that, but had the sense that the comment by the neighbor made him lose interest in his body and he moved on.

"What do you make of that?" asked Ted.

"I honestly don't know," I said. "I just don't have a clue."

"Get your nose out of that stupid magazine!"

A woman named Dena told me the story of a shared death experience she had while caring for a "distant great-aunt," by which she meant a relative who had never been close to the family. As Dena put it, "We drew straws for who would take care of her and I lost."

The two days before her great-aunt died were tough on Dena. The great-aunt was "prattling out of her head" about dead relatives, talking to them as if they were there in the room.

"I thought she was demented and all I wanted to do was get away from her because it made me uncomfortable," said Dena. Rather than try to provide comfort, Dena bought a stack of celebrity magazines at the hospital newsstand and buried her nose in them. On the day her great-aunt would die, Dena was absorbed in the pages of *People* magazine, ignoring the woman, who was unconscious and only hours from death. All of a sudden Dena distinctly heard her great-aunt speak. "I was surprised to hear her, because I really thought she was long gone," said the young woman.

"I said, get your face out of that stupid magazine and look at what's happening to me!" said the woman with a surprisingly strong voice.

Dena looked up and found herself face-to-face with her deceased grandmother. The woman Dena saw was much younger than when Dena had last seen her and far more self-assured than when she was alive. Dena had a million things she wanted to ask her grandmother, but before she could speak, her grandmother disappeared.

From that point until she died, Dena's great-aunt was coherent. For the last few hours of her life, Dena and her great-aunt spoke as if they had been close friends for decades. It was a conversation, by the way, that included the late grandmother. At nine that night, the great-aunt died, leaving Dena sorry that she had not had a relationship with her all those years. It also left her with a question that she asked me at the end of her story.

"Why, Dr. Moody, would I have this experience with someone that I didn't even care about?"

"Do these always make people happier?"

A Canadian doctor told me about an event that happened to him more than thirty years ago, when he was doing his residency in internal medicine. The doctor, whom I'll call Gordon, had a patient named Mr. Parker, an affable man who looked much older than his years because he was suffering from chronic obstructive pulmonary disease (COPD), a breathing disease caused by cigarette smoking.

Gordon got to know Mr. Parker during his several hospitalizations. Mr. Parker was a good talker with a colorful life and soon became one of Gordon's favorite patients. If he had a few extra minutes to spend with patients, Gordon would visit Mr. Parker and listen to his tales of Montreal, where the two lived.

During one of his hospitalizations, Mr. Parker asked to be released a few days early so he could spend the Christmas holidays with his family. Gordon didn't feel completely comfortable with that request since Mr. Parker was having difficulty breathing, but Gordon decided to let him go anyway.

A few days after Christmas, while Gordon was on call, he came around the corner of a hallway in the emergency room to find Mr. Parker looking down the hall.

"He was standing there quietly, looking at something that I could not see because he was looking down the hall the other way, perpendicular to my line of sight," said

Gordon. "He seemed curious, but impassive. I spoke to him and he looked at me and lit up. I say lit up intentionally because he really did. There was a light of sorts that emanated from him—a clear light—and I felt like I was seeing into his soul."

Gordon turned and could see that Mr. Parker was looking at a dead body on a gurney that was covered by a sheet. Gordon peeled back the sheet and could see that the body Mr. Parker was looking at was his own! "I looked at Mr. Parker and could hear his voice in thoughts that I understood were coming from him," said Gordon. "He insisted to me that he was not that body and I wasn't to be concerned about him. All this came in thoughts, not words, but I understood them clearly. There is no misunderstanding when you are in this situation."

Gordon looked directly at Mr. Parker. The COPD patient was no longer struggling for breath. Rather, said Gordon, there was a feeling of "emphatic joy" rushing through the area around his body.

"I had a feeling of other people in a semicircle closing around Mr. Parker," said Gordon. "There seemed to be a kind of energy rolling back and forth between Mr. Parker's form and these unseen presences that were gathering around."

Gordon stared at Mr. Parker until—"in a flash"—his patients disappeared in a field of "bright golden light." "I could see several layers in this transparent golden light and for a moment there was a shower of bright golden specks," said Gordon. "These specks reminded me of the sea spray that is tossed up by a wave crashing at the beach. These shining specks were a cloud around me but it was only an instant."

When I spoke to Gordon, he said that he had been a "changed man" ever since that experience. From that day forward, said Gordon, he'd had no trepidations about death—his or anyone else's.

"My medical colleagues comment about how composed I always seem," said Gordon. "But as you might imagine I do not share this experience with them. I just leave them to wonder why I am always blissed out."

From Gordon, the question was a general one. "Do experiences like these always make people happier?"

"Why doesn't it happen every time?"

In Winston-Salem, North Carolina, I met a hospice counselor named David, who had both witnessed and heard many shared death experiences. Among the most impressive was a man who was on deathbed watch with his wife, who was dying from pancreatic cancer.

As he held her in her final moments, a bright light filled the room that stunned the hospice worker. Even now, as he attempted to describe it, words failed. He saw it as "the brightest light I'd ever seen," yet at the same time, something that seemed more like "plasma or the kind of light you see when you get snow-blinded."

This light was present for everyone in the room, said David, but this man had a particularly vivid experience.

As he was holding his wife when she passed away, he felt himself racing up a tunnel as she died. Then, he told David, he could feel her pass through him and into a bright light that glowed at the end of the tunnel.

"I knew I couldn't go any further," he told David as they all sat next to his deceased wife. "I wanted to, but something kept me from going beyond the end of the tunnel."

Later, this man's mother was dying in the hospice and he was there every day. "I hope it happens again with my mother," he told David. Unfortunately for the man, it didn't.

"He expected it to happen every time, I guess, and he was quite disappointed when it didn't happen with his mother." At which point David looked at me and asked the obvious: "Why *doesn't* it happen every time?"

"A golden ball of light"

After one book signing, a young man from Georgia approached me with an astounding story about the death of his grandfather. The young man said that his grandfather had farmed the same land all of his life. So when he became ill, he insisted on staying there at the farmhouse until, as he put it, "they carry me out feet first."

The family members agreed to that arrangement and everyone took turns sitting with Grandpa in his final days. On the day that the young man had bedside duty, it became clear that his grandfather would not make it much longer. The young man was mentally prepared. He sat next to his grandfather's bed and talked to the old man until it appeared he had stopped breathing. When the young man put his hand on his grandfather's chest to check his heartbeat, he suddenly felt very strange, as though the room was closing in and the walls had turned to rubber.

Then, without warning, the young man found himself standing "in a scene" from his grandfather's life. "The farm and the animals were around us, and I was in the scenes of his life as they flowed through like a wind sweeping by," he said to me. "I was able to communicate with my grandfather at the same time. It was clear to me that his death and this moment marked the end of an era."

But that wasn't all that happened, said the young man. When his grandfather died, the young man was astounded to see a "golden ball of light" rise from his chest and pass through the ceiling.

What he said left me stammering. I didn't know what to say, and I guess he recognized that fact. "I read your book, Dr. Moody, hoping that it would give me some kind of idea about what had happened," said the young man. "But there were no experiences that were like the one that happened to me."

"Strange but not creepy"

In Los Angeles, a well-known movie producer I will call Sarah offered a shared experience that seemed ripe for the big screen.

Sarah was on the East Coast visiting her boyfriend. Early in the morning, she said she began to feel uneasy and found it nearly impossible to get back to sleep. ("You know, the feeling you get when you think something is happening somewhere that you are supposed to know about.") As the feeling intensified, she began to think about members of her family, racing through thoughts of each one. Sarah paused at her father. For no particular reason she began to think that maybe he was in trouble or needed some kind of help.

She began to toss and turn, and as she did her boyfriend came in and said that he, too, was having difficultly sleeping. They began to talk, and as they did they saw her father hovering over her bed "like a ghost!" They both froze and looked at her father for several moments.

"It was strange but not creepy," said the producer. "I looked at him for signs of distress or some other reason that he was there, but I just couldn't figure it out. Then it dawned on me that he was certainly dead and he wanted to tell me himself. We had a strong bond, so it seemed perfectly sensible to me."

Before long, the "spiritual image," as she called it, faded away and the two were left to puzzle about the incredible visitation.

After about twenty minutes, Sarah received a telephone call from her mother with the painful but not surprising news that her father had died.

"I know it seems strange, but it really wasn't," said the producer. "But I am the one who was close to my father. My boyfriend didn't even know him. The thing I want to know is, why was my boyfriend able to experience my father's death in the same way I did?"

"A figment of our imagination?"

A woman at a conference in upstate New York told me about being at her mother's bedside when she died. Sally was now in her seventies, but the events of that night poured out of her as though they had happened only days earlier. Here is what she had to say:

"The first thing that happened when my mother passed was the light changed intensity and grew much brighter real fast. All kinds of things started happening at once, such as a kind of rocking motion that went through my whole body. It was like my whole body rocked forward one time real quick and then instantly I was seeing the room from a different angle from above and to the left side of the bed instead of the right side. It was like I was viewing my mother's body from the wrong side according to where I was stationed in the room.

"This rocking forward motion was very comfortable, and not at all like a shudder and especially not like when a car you are riding in lurches to the side and you get nauseous. I did not feel uncomfortable but in fact the opposite; I felt far more comfortable and peaceful than I ever felt in my life.

"I don't know whether I was out of my body or not because all the other things that were going on held my attention. I was just glued to scenes from my mother's life that were flashing throughout the room or around the bed. I cannot even tell whether the room was there anymore or if it was, there was a

whole section of it I hadn't noticed before. I would compare it to the surprise you would have if you had lived in the same house for many years, but one day you opened up a closet and found a big secret compartment you didn't know about. This thing seemed so strange and yet perfectly natural at the same time.

"The scenes that were flashing around in midair contained things that had happened to my mother, some of which I remembered but others I didn't. I could see her looking at the scenes too, and she sure recognized all of them, as I could tell by her expression as she watched. This all happened at once so there is no way of telling it that matches the situation.

"The scenes of my mother's life reminded me of old-fashioned flashbulbs going off. When they did, I saw scenes of her life like in one of the 3-D movies of the 1950s.

"By the time the flashes of her life were going on, she was out of her body. I saw my father, who passed seven years before, standing there where the head of the bed would have been. By this point the bed was kind of irrelevant and my father was coaching my mother out of her body.

"That was amusing because in life he had been a football coach at the high school I attended. Frankly, I felt a little disappointed that he still had that coaching mentality, as if he had not moved on to better things since his death.

"I looked right into his face and a recognition of love passed between us, but he went right back to focusing on my mother. He looked like a young man, although he was seventy-nine when he died. There was a glow about him or all through him—very vibrant. He was full of life.

"One of his favorite expressions was 'Look alive!' and he sure did look alive when he was coaching my mother out of her body.

A part of her that was transparent just stood right up, going through her body, and she and my father glided off into the light and disappeared.

"The room sort of rocked again, or my body did, but this time backward in the opposite direction and then everything went back to normal.

"I felt great tenderness from my mother and father. This entire event overflowed with love and kindness. Since that day I wonder: Is the world we live in just a figment of our imagination?"

"This is what death is"

Juan, a very intense man in his thirties, approached me at a conference in Spain with a story about the death of his much older brother. He and his sister-in-law were in the living room of her house when the older brother walked into the room, stumbled and collapsed on the floor. Juan pulled his brother onto the sofa while his sister-in-law called emergency services and waited on the doorstep for them to arrive.

Juan hovered over his brother, who suddenly went from being extremely distressed to extraordinarily calm. A smile of peace and serenity came over his face, which frightened Juan.

Suddenly, Juan felt himself lift out of his body and look down on the scene below, which consisted of him hovering over his brother's body. From this perspective near the ceiling, Juan could see his brother leave his body in a sort of "clear light" that rose from his chest and moved rapidly away. Juan said he knew his brother was saying good-bye to him, but he could not say that he heard the words through his ears; rather he only heard them in his head.

With his brother gone, Juan faced another dilemma; he couldn't get back into his body. At first he panicked. Then he relaxed and enjoyed it. "This is what death is," he told himself, reveling in this unique visual perspective.

Finally, when emergency services arrived, Juan returned to his body. He began to laugh when that happened.

"The emergency-service people were surprised to find me laughing over my brother's dead body," said Juan. "I didn't tell them what had happened because they would have taken me to the hospital instead of my brother."

"What has been the effect on you?" I asked.

"I am more calm now than I used to be," he said.

"More calm? You seem very intense to me!"

Juan shrugged. "You should have seen me then. I was really bad news."

"Did I really go to heaven?"

A housewife approached me after a book signing in Atlanta to tell me a story about her sister. This woman—I'll call her Gail—had nursed her sister through chemotherapy for breast cancer. When the chemotherapy didn't work and the cancer spread, she was with her sister daily until she died.

At the moment of her sister's death, Gail witnessed a "halo" of "tiny light particles" that gathered around her chest and her head. "I actually felt her leave her body," said Gail. "I leaned over to hug her and felt her pass through me like a pulse of energy. It was genuinely an outburst of happiness and release."

Gail said that she "lingered" with her sister as she died. "I walked part way over with her to the afterlife," she said. "When I leaned over to hug her, I could tell that she was dead and there was no more bodily voice, but we didn't need one. We could pass thoughts back and forth without speaking."

As they continued to communicate telepathically with one another, Gail said she noticed they were floating, "but in a space with no walls." And although she did not see their parents, she had the feeling that they were there along with an uncle who had recently died.

"I lingered in this place for a while," she said. "I felt her pull away from me and that was it—she was gone to heaven and I came back."

"That's an amazing story," I said.

Gail agreed.

"Since then I have not been upset about death. I didn't even cry at my sister's funeral. But I can't help but wonder: Did I really go to heaven?"

✧✧✧

"They just swirled out of the room"

A gentleman named Dave approached me at a book-signing event in Seattle to tell me about the shared death experience he'd had with his wife several years earlier. She had just completed a round of chemotherapy and was not feeling well. There was no reason to expect her to die anytime soon, said Dave, which is why he was so surprised to hear her voice as he stood in the kitchen.

"I knew she was dying because I could hear her talking directly into my ear," he said. "She was saying, 'I've just died, but that's okay. Everything is fine. Please don't worry.'"

Dave walked into the bedroom and found what he feared: his wife lying dead in bed. What he didn't expect to see was his wife's mother, leaning over her daughter and welcoming her to the other side. "Her mother had died thirty years earlier, and I saw their bond renew right before my eyes," said Dave. The mother and daughter hugged and then "swirled up and out of the room."

It was a great relief to Dave, who said that there was cheerfulness in his wife's voice that "lifts me up and keeps me going every day."

Questions and more questions

"All good scientific studies lead to more questions than answers."

I wrote that sentence in one of the notebooks where I collected stories of shared death experiences, near-death

experiences and other spiritual events told to me by people who'd had them and wanted their meaning explained.

I wanted to understand them too. Of all the aspects of
the near-death experience that I could have researched, I
found myself most interested in shared death experiences.
That is saying a lot, given that some of the other elements
include out-of-body experiences, in which an individual
leaves his or her body at the point of death and is able
to witness his or her own resuscitation or even events in
other rooms; panoramic life reviews, in which the person
near death relives his or her entire life in vivid detail; trips
up the tunnel; or seeing dead relatives and beings that are
often described as God or Jesus.

Every aspect of the near-death experience interests me.
But the shared death experience became the most puzzling. To me, a shared death experience provided an opportunity like no other to address a number of questions
that have plagued mankind since the beginning. Some
of these questions are obvious, and some are not. For
example:

- Mankind has always suspected the existence of an
  "afterlife portal," an entryway that opens into the
  spiritual world. Some people call these the "Pearly
  Gates." I have heard a number of case studies in which
  a portal opens and the individuals involved in the
  shared death experience are absorbed. Do shared death
  experiences tell us anything about the portal discussed
  so often through history?
- Has nature provided us with the equipment to communicate with the divine? In other words, is there a

"God module" in each of our brains? Near-death experiences indicate that such mental equipment might exist. Shared death experiences allow the notion of a God module to be explored even further.

- Shared death experiences may prove the existence of a heavenly plane. One of the arguments of skeptics of the near-death experience is that they are "fear-death" experiences made up in the mind of a person who is facing death. I think shared death experiences could prove that the light and all of the good things that come from it originate *outside* of the dying person's brain, where others can share them. This phenomenon, known as *non-local memory*, involves personal information that resides outside of an individual's brain.

Many other questions have come up about shared death experiences because *all good science leads to more questions than answers.* I continued to collect shared death experience case studies over the years, and as I did so, I continued to collect my thoughts about the subject as well.

And then something happened that greatly accelerated my interest in shared death experiences: My mother died and *I* had one.

"We are not human beings having a spiritual experience. We are spiritual beings having a human experience."

—PIERRE DE CHARDIN

3

✧✧✧

An Experience of My Own

It was May 8, 1994, Mother's Day, and I was at a public telephone in a shopping mall in Las Vegas. I was attending a conference at the University of Nevada, Las Vegas, on shared death experiences. After years of collecting the case studies of shared death experiences and considering their implications, I was about to launch a study that would examine the phenomenon, breaking them down into their component parts to try to figure out why and how they took place. The implications were clear: that death opens a portal to the "other side." By now I had faith that such a portal does exist. But obviously this supposition needed further evaluation. Faith alone gets you very little in the world of research.

At any rate, because it was Mother's Day, I temporarily left the conference and went to the mall with my family.

While there, I stopped at a pay phone to call my mother. She was seventy-four years old and still lived in the first house that she and my father owned, in Macon, Georgia. As I dialed her telephone number, I had no problem imagining her sitting in the living room, reading the most recent issue of *Guideposts* magazine and waiting for her children to call.

"Well, hello, Raymond," she said. "I knew you would call me today."

Conversation with my mother had always been a great comfort to me. In fact, I have always been a devout mama's boy, and truth be told, a man who enjoys the company of women more than men.

That attitude toward women has a lot to do with my upbringing. I was born on June 30, 1944, the very day that my father shipped out for World War II. I don't know what my mother was thinking as she labored to give birth to me that summer day. Given the way her life had gone up to that point, she probably thought that her husband would be killed in the war and never see his newborn son. Eight of her fifteen brothers and sisters had died in childhood, and one more would be lost in the war. Death had been a constant companion for Mom, and it would be safe to say that she didn't expect the future to be any different.

I know mine was a difficult birth. Mom was young, I was large, and negative thoughts about her husband's likelihood of returning from a very violent war were on her mind as she struggled with childbirth.

The pains of labor, the dark memories, and the fear of the future all added up to a tremendous case of depression, which my young mother would only talk about with her parents. In those days, people didn't speak freely about their emotions as they do now. Americans were almost devoutly stoic, expected to show quiet endurance in the face of adversity rather than let anyone know how they truly felt. The result for my mother was a worsening case of depression, one that she had to hold inside rather than express.

I think the town of Porterdale, Georgia, was filled with women coping with anxiety and sadness similar to my mother's. World War II had emptied the town of all its young men, and the women of Porterdale lived with daily doubts that their sons, husbands and lovers would come home alive.

The war also left many of them childless. Few children had been born since the United States entered the war in 1941. And now, with my birth in 1944, an event of some importance had occurred in the town of Porterdale. There was a new baby.

That was good for my mother. When she needed a rest or just some time alone, her parents would take over the role of parenting. They doted on me as if I were the only child they had ever seen, passing me constantly from one to the other in an effort to give my mother breathing space. It was through them that I was "shared out" to the rest of the community, an arrangement that gave me a large and caring family of very loving women.

All of the women in the neighborhood who were about the age of my grandmother unofficially adopted me as a grandchild of their own. Two doors down was

Mrs. Crowell. She became one of the most important figures in my life. I remember her as being a sweet but very
strong woman, the kind I would eventually be most happy
with in marriage. I would go see her all the time—as a
child and later as a teen. She allowed me to enter her home
without even knocking, which I did frequently. Once inside, I would curl up on her sofa and dream. She was
among the most encouraging people in my life. Her son
told me at her funeral years later that when I was an in-
fant she would hold me on her lap and repeat over and
over to me, "Raymond, you are going to be a very special
person someday."

All of the women in town were encouraging and
loving. It was through them—but especially through my
mother—that I developed empathy, my most valuable
personal and professional trait. After all, a psychiatrist
without empathy is of little use to his patients.

Anyway, on this Mother's Day in 1994, I stood in the
mall talking to my mom and remembering a lifetime of
great times together. She told me what my brothers and
sisters were doing and recounted events in the neighborhood. Before long I realized that I had been on the phone
for almost an hour.

"Mom, I have to go now. I was supposed to meet Cheryl
(my wife) twenty minutes ago and I don't want her to wait
too long," I said. "One more thing: How are you doing?"

"Oh, I'm fine," she said very cheerfully. "Yesterday I
got a rash on my arms but Kay (my sister) took me to the
emergency room and the doctor there said it was nothing.
So I'm about as good as I can be."

I questioned her more about the rash but there wasn't much else to say. "The ER doctor got me an appointment with a dermatologist tomorrow and we'll see what he says," she told me. "I don't expect that it amounts to much."

I wish she had been right.

A deadly prognosis and strange events

The next day I received a tearful phone call from my sister. She had gone to the dermatologist with Mom and watched as his pleasant demeanor turned to one of great concern. She knew there were problems when he ordered some tests and demanded immediate results back from the lab. That afternoon, looking drained, the dermatologist rendered his diagnosis with no embellishments.

"Mrs. Moody, you have non-Hodgkin's lymphoma," he said. "You have two days to two weeks to live."

This cancer of the white blood cells can be very fast growing, and according to the oncologist, hers was the fastest-growing possible—"fulminate," as the doctor declared. "I'm terribly sorry."

I knew what this meant. The cancer was spreading so fast that chemotherapy would have little effect on its progression. We flew immediately to Macon, Georgia, and for the next two weeks we joined the rest of the Moody family in making her final days as comfortable as possible. We stayed at her side for the last few days she was at home and then we all moved into the hospital and stayed with her until she died, which was two weeks to the day from when she was given her fatal diagnosis.

The day she died, we all gathered around the bed. She had been comatose for the last two days, but shortly before she passed she awoke and with great coherency told us that she loved us all very much.

"Please say that again, Momma?" asked my sister Kay.

With great effort Mom batted her oxygen mask away and said it again: "I love you all very much."

It was a touching moment for us all, one that built false hope that she was perhaps recovering but also emphasized the powerful need she had to express love just one more time.

We all held hands around the bed—my two sisters, their husbands, and Cheryl and I—and waited for the inevitable moment of death.

And as we waited, it happened to us: a shared death experience. As we held hands around the bed, the room seemed to change shape and four of the six of us felt as though we were being lifted off the ground. I had the feeling that the room had turned into the shape of an hourglass. I felt a strong pull, like a riptide that was pulling me out to sea, only the pull was upward.

"Look," said my sister, pointing to a spot at the end of the bed. "Dad's here! He's come back to get her!"

Everyone there reported later that the light in the room changed to a soft and fuzzy texture. It was like looking at light in a swimming pool at night.

As all of this took place, there was great joy in the room. We all knew something truly incredible had happened to all of us as our mother died. It was as though the fabric of the universe had torn and for just a moment we felt the energy of that place called heaven.

After the funeral we spent a few more days in Macon with my family, taking care of the loose ends that are always left after a death. It was during this period of time that we all began to compare our experiences at Mom's bedside and realized how extraordinary they had been. We were all convinced by our individual experiences that we had each shared Mom's death in a unique, spiritual way. My brother-in-law, the Reverend Rick Lanford, a Methodist minister, summed it up best when he said, "I felt like I left my physical body and went into another plane with her. It was like nothing that had ever happened to me."

I agreed completely with Rick. We all did. What should have been one of life's least happy moments was suddenly cause for elation. We had gone partway to heaven with our mother. We had personally seen her off to heaven!

More questions than answers

From that point on I noticed the beginnings of a phenomenon: More people were asking me about shared death experiences than were asking about near-death experiences. This happened first through my mail and e-mail correspondence. Then questions began to come up in personal conversations. At lectures and conferences, people would ask me if I had ever heard of near-death experiences taking place with people who were not dying, but were attending to someone who was. The scales had clearly tipped. The Baby-Boom Generation was gaining familiarity with death as parents and loved ones were passing on. With this trend came more opportunity for shared death experiences. Since baby boomers were the open generation, they were willing to talk about almost anything, including strange happenings at the deathbed.

As an experiment I included a description of shared death experiences in the lectures I delivered at various conferences around the world. "Shared death experiences are like near-death experiences, only they take place in a person who is not ill," I might say. "They usually happen to a person or persons who are sitting at a deathbed and they take place when the sick person is close to death or has just died. They can happen to one or more people. If they happen to a group, the spiritual experiences they describe later are remarkably similar."

After offering this description, I would ask how many in the crowd had had such an experience. To my surprise, anywhere from 5 to 10 percent of every audience would hold up their hands. This was an astounding amount, especially considering that it was only slightly less than the number who raised their hands when asked if they'd had near-death experiences. *How things have changed*, I thought. Since the fine work of Kübler-Ross in the seventies, many more people have been allowed to sit at the bedsides of their dying loved ones.

It was this rise in the number of shared death experiences—and my own such experience—that drew me back to its study. Over the course of the next several years I wrote down more questions in my notebook. I then looked for case studies that would best illustrate them and perhaps help answer them. Why did I do that? Because near-death research has always been a study of stories. This is both the beauty of working in this field and its frustration. Through stories we are able to know the elements of a near-death experience. But despite the beauty of these stories—some of which are touching beyond belief—the frustration is that they don't usually happen in a clinical setting when medical researchers know they are taking place. Therefore, they can't be observed like a heart attack or fever. Science requires experiments to be designed so that they can be reproduced over and over again under controlled conditions. These experiments must be such that other scientists can achieve the same results. Unfortunately, these death-related experiences don't lend themselves to being reproduced, unless, of course, ghoulish measures were to be implemented, like stopping and starting a subject's heart or otherwise inducing near-death.

Near-death and shared death experiences are subjective events, ones that can be seen and interpreted only by the beholder. For this reason, the stories are so crucial to this work. They are the best evidence we have.

With that in mind, I combined the questions posed in the previous chapter with further questions. My goal was to ask all of the important questions that could be asked about shared death experiences, thereby getting a dialogue started about their mysteries. I also intended to break them down into their common elements, which is very important for the study of any human phenomenon; it was only after naming the near-death experience and then deconstructing it into its common elements that the field of near-death studies could begin. The common elements of a phenomenon are like a roadmap for future research.

Drawing on resources for answers

To answer these questions and to dissect shared death experiences into their common elements, I chose to rely on the resources of others, and not just mine alone. I had been collecting dozens of shared death experiences but I was not alone in that endeavor. Other researchers were finding them as well. The fact that they were doing this was a good thing. If several people can't observe a phenomenon or have patients describe it independently, then it most likely doesn't exist. As Robert Green Ingersoll, the nineteenth-century American orator, said, "Reason, observation and experience are the Holy Trinity of science."

Despite the collection of stories that was taking place among my fellow researchers, none had truly launched into a study of why and how these incidents had taken place. And no one had truly broken down the shared death experience into its elements, which was among my most ambitious goals. Still, they were collecting stories that could help.

With the care that only time and observation can provide, I began to explore these questions and to match them with case studies from shared death experiencers. As I framed these questions, the importance of the shared death experience to the broader study of our intuitive consciousness became crystal clear.

Can we communicate with the divine?

The human brain is known to some as "the three-pound universe," a reference to its weight. I look at it differently. The brain is a three-pound planet, perhaps, but it's the mind that is our universe. The French philosopher Descartes said that the mind is "all things that are not matter," by which I think he surely meant "gray matter." The mind is what the brain does. It is the center of consciousness, the indefinable parts of the brain that generate thoughts, feelings, ideas and our communication with the world.

I think it's the mind that gives us the ability to communicate with God and the spiritual world, and it is the realization of that spiritual world that defines us more than anything as human beings.

Science is always looking for ways to define us as human beings. For example, it was the widely accepted notion for some time that we were the only tool users in the animal kingdom. The ability to recognize that life could be made easier with tools pointed to our superiority. But the tool hypothesis was disproved in recent years as several different animals have been shown to use tools to gather food.

The one true difference between humans and the rest of the animal kingdom is that we emphasize a sense of mortality and a belief in a spiritual life. We bury our dead in a ritualistic way, believe in an afterlife (at least most of us do), and use our minds to communicate with God. There is something within the human mind that needs to commune with a higher power.

Carl Jung believed that the need to commune with God was completely natural and not neurotic, as his contemporary Sigmund Freud declared. That may have been because Jung had a near-death experience in 1944, one that took him "high up in space" and then brought him back to earth, where it seemed his ego and all of the other baggage of life were stripped from him, allowing him to examine the core of himself for what he was. He wrote beautifully about his near-death experience, which took place as a result of a serious heart attack. Here is part of what he wrote in his autobiography, *Memories, Dreams, Reflections*:

[A] strange thing happened: I had the feeling that everything was being sloughed away; everything I aimed at or wished for or thought, the whole phantasmagoria of earthly existence, fell away or was stripped from me—an extremely painful process. Nevertheless something remained; it was as if I now carried along with me everything I had ever experienced or done, everything that had happened around me. I might also say: it was with me, and I was it. I consisted of all that, so to speak. I consisted of my own history and I felt with great certainty: this is what I am. I am this bundle of what has been and what has been accomplished.

This experience gave me a feeling of extreme poverty, but at the same time of great fullness. There was no longer anything I wanted or desired. I existed in an objective form; I was what I had been and lived. At first the sense of annihilation predominated, of having been stripped or pillaged; but suddenly that became of no consequence.

Everything seemed to be past; what remained was a fait accompli, without any reference back to what had been. There was no longer any regret that something had dropped away or been taken away. On the contrary: I had everything that I was, and that was everything . . .

In reality, a good three weeks were still to pass before I could truly make up my mind to live again. I could not eat because all food repelled me. The view of city and mountains from my sickbed seemed to me like a painted curtain with black holes in it, or a tattered sheet of newspaper full of photographs that meant nothing. Disappointed, I thought, "Now I must return to the 'box system' again." For it seemed to me as if behind the horizon of the cosmos a three-dimensional world had been artificially built up, in which each person sat by himself in a little box. And now I should have to convince myself all over again that this was important! Life and the whole world struck me as a prison, and it bothered me beyond measure that I should again be finding all that quite in order. I had been so glad to shed it all, and now it had come about that I—along with everyone else—would again be hung up in a box by a thread.

After this incredible experience, Jung wrote that it was perfectly normal to think of life after death, and not neurotic at all. Instead he said that it's the neurotics who try to push thoughts of the afterlife and God out of their minds.

"The unconscious psyche believes in life after death," he wrote, just around the time that he had a shared death experience, this with one of his wife's cousins.

"I dreamed that my wife's bed was a deep pit with stone walls. It was a grave, and somehow had a suggestion of classical antiquity about it. Then I head a deep sigh, as if someone were giving up the ghost. A figure that resembled my wife sat up in the pit and floated upward. It wore a white gown into which curious black symbols were woven. I awoke, roused my wife, and checked the time. It was three o'clock in the morning. The dream was so curious that I thought at once that it might signify a death. At seven o'clock came the news that a cousin of my wife had died at three o'clock in the morning."

In Jung's mind it was not curious at all to think that we had the ability to communicate with God. In an essay entitled "On Life After Death," Jung wrote that at least part of the psyche is not subject to the laws of space and time. A complete view of the world would require another dimension, he wrote. Then and only then could life be given a "unified explanation."

"We must face the fact that our world, with its time, space and causality, relates to another order of things lying behind or beneath it, in which neither 'here and there' nor 'earlier and later' are of importance. I have been convinced that at least a part of our psychic existence is characterized by a relativity of space and time. This relativity seems to increase, in proportion to the distance from consciousness, to an absolute condition of timelessness and spacelessness."

Jung was a great observer and certainly a believer in our ability to communicate with the other side. He believed this happened through "the aid of hints" that come to us in dreams as well as when we are near death.

When Jung referred to being "near death," he meant, of course, our own deaths. But shared death experiences have taught me that being near death can certainly mean the deaths of others. There is something about being in the presence of death—not necessarily our own—that can open a portal to a higher world, one that those who are dying can open to those who will go on living.

In studying shared death experience we hear people say "a window opened and I saw heaven," or "the room seemed to change shape and I could follow my mother into the other world," or "it was like a door that opened itself and I could just go in with my wife." Perfectly lucid people see this portal to the other side and are able to communicate with the divine through it.

This leads to an entirely different question, and perhaps one of the most interesting of all in dealing with shared death experiences.

✧✧✧

Does a shared memory exist?

Can memory be stored outside of the body? If it can, can we access it through shared death experiences? Philosophers and scientists alike have long pondered the question of memory existing outside of the body. The notion that this may happen is supported by Harvard University research showing that rats with 50 percent of their brains removed could run mazes as well as rats with 100 percent of their brains intact. This study led the chief researcher, Dr. Karl Lashley, to say, "If I didn't know better, I would think that memory is stored outside of the brain." So if memory can reside outside of the brain, how do we get to it?

My research indicates that shared death experiences may be one of the ways in which this information is accessed. In many shared death experiences, we hear the witness say that they saw portions of the dying person's life that they could never have known about. There are examples of this throughout this book, but this particularly striking example comes from *Parting Visions*, a book written by fellow researcher Melvin Morse, MD, and my co-author, Paul Perry. This is the story of Olga Gearhardt, the late matriarch of a large family in San Diego.

In 1988, a virus attacked Olga's heart, leaving it so weak that it could no longer beat effectively. The only chance she had for survival was a heart transplant. I'll let the excerpt carry the rest of the story:

Olga was put on the transplant-recipient list at the University of California Medical Center. People who are on this list must be in constant contact with the hospital where the transplant will be done. If a heart becomes available that matches their blood type, it must be implanted within hours of the donor's death for the transplant to be effective.

Olga's entire family was notified of this fact, and they all promised to lend moral support by being there at the hospital during her surgery. Early in 1989 Olga received the call from the hospital that a matching heart had been found. As she and her husband left for the hospital, her children started a telephone chain to notify family members in three states that the transplant was about to begin. In a matter of hours the waiting room of the hospital was overloaded with Olga's family.

The only member of the family not at the hospital was Olga's son-in-law. Although he loved his mother-in-law, he had a phobia about hospitals and preferred to await news at home.

Late that evening her chest was opened and the transplant was performed successfully. At 2:15 AM she developed unexpected complications, and the new heart would not beat properly. As the medical personnel became alarmed, the heart suddenly stopped beating altogether. It took a long period of resuscitation before the heart finally began functioning properly. Meanwhile the family in the waiting room was told nothing about these complications, and most of them were asleep. About six in the morning the family was told that the operation was a success but that she had almost died when the new heart failed.

Olga's daughter immediately called her husband to tell him the good news. "I know she's okay," he said. "She already told me herself."

He had awakened at 2:15 AM to see his mother-in-law standing at the foot of his bed. "It was as though she was standing right there," he said. Thinking she had not had surgery and had somehow come to his house instead, he sat up and asked her how she was.

"I am fine, I'm going to be all right," she said. "There is nothing for any of us to worry about." Then she disappeared.

The vision didn't frighten the son-in-law, but he did get out of bed and write down the time she appeared to him and exactly what was said.

When the family went in to see her, Olga began talking about "the strange dream" that took place during surgery. She said she had left her body and watched the doctors work on her for a few minutes. Then she went into the waiting room, where she saw her family. Frustrated by her inability to communicate with them, she decided to travel to her daughter's home, about thirty miles away, and connect with her son-in-law.

She told them that she was sure she had stood at the foot of her son-in-law's bed and told him that everything was going to be all right.

"There is no way to dismiss this story as an hallucination or as a phenomenon of a chemically imbalanced brain," wrote Morse. He and Perry spent a considerable amount of time interviewing family members to determine if there were any discrepancies in fact. There were none.

As Morse wrote: "The only explanation is this: During the time this woman was on a heart-lung machine because her new heart was not functioning properly, she was able to leave her body and communicate with her son-in-law, who was in bed more than thirty miles away."

Granted, this and similar stories in this book may be examples of telepathy. But they may also well be examples of memory residing outside of a person's brain and in the fabric of the universe, where it becomes available under certain conditions, shared death experiences being one. Some researchers call this a "participatory universe," defined as one in which life and mind are woven into the fabric of the universe. In theory, they say, memories are stored all around us.

Some near-death experience researchers say that this "memory fabric" explains how memories, feelings and sensations are experienced simultaneously during a life review. And since this fabric contains the memories of many, those who die and then return to life are also able to feel the effects of their journey on the pivotal people in their lives.

If this "memory fabric" theory were correct, then a person sharing another's death experience would most certainly tap into the same memory bank and be able to experience the same events as the person dying. It is the universal quality of this memory bank that led a child in one of my cohorts' research to call this place of memory "the house of God."

Thinking of the house of God reminds me of the story of Linda Jacquin, president of her own advertising firm in Wentzville, Missouri. At the age of seven, Linda tapped into this memory bank after having eye surgery, which left her bandaged and sightless for several days while recovering in the hospital. Here is her description of what happened:

"I had just had surgery on my eyes and was in the hospital. My eyes were bandaged and I couldn't see anything. As a result, my other senses had become very acute. I could hear the muffled voices of the nurses and doctors at the nursing station as they talked about the various patients, and the squeaking sound of the gum-soled shoes as the nurses walked by was extraordinarily loud.

"As I lay frightened in my bed, I suddenly saw a light and out of that light came a boy named Jimmy, who was one of my elementary-school classmates. He was a sweet boy and he came up to me through the light and said, 'Linda, I can't find my way home. Can you walk me home?'

"'Of course I can,' I said, and we walked into the light until we got to his house.

"'Thanks,' said Jimmy, and then he kept walking alone as I stopped and watched.

"I later found out that Jimmy had been struck by a car and killed on the same day that I had my surgery."

Vivid experiences like that of Linda's may well be examples of telepathy, which I deal with just ahead in this chapter. Or there may be some other quality in the shared death experience that brings a person into contact with the memory fabric of the universe. Either way—telepathy or a universal shared memory—the result can be a shared death experience.

✦✦✦

Does telepathy exist?

Almost everyone has examples of "telepathy" in everyday life. Science has shown that groups of people who live together often think so much alike that they can frequently finish one another's sentences or tell what another person is thinking before they are told. Some scientists even speculate that good teamwork consists largely of telepathic abilities to know what is needed to make the team *work* as one.

There are the stories about twins living in different parts of the world who send the same Mother's Day card to their mother, or who call home at almost precisely the same time as their siblings.

And then, of course, husbands and wives often know what their spouse is thinking. Or ...

You get the picture. Evidence of telepathy is all around us. And although it can often be written off to chance, telepathic events frequently go far out of the realm of chance and into the paranormal.

One great example comes from Sussanna Uballe, who wrote in an online journal about sharing the death experience of her husband, who was murdered at a store while Sussanna slept at home. Here, in Sussanna's own words, is her story:

"I did not have a near-death experience, but I did travel partway up the tunnel with my husband as he left this dimension.

"On Memorial Day 1979, I was five months pregnant. My husband and I rode bicycles and ran errands around town, and it was a very hot day for Minneapolis. I lay down after dinner and was so exhausted that I could barely move. As my husband went to the corner store at 8:00 PM to buy something for his lunch the next day, I fell into a very deep sleep.

"I dreamt that I was walking with my husband, Herb, up a dark and shady forest path. It was a heavily wooded path, which was enclosed by a thick canopy of trees overhead. The path was slightly inclined, and at the crest of a hill I saw the sky, somewhat like the light at the end of a tunnel. Herb and I had been in deep conversation, about what I could not tell, but I suppose we were reminiscing about our relationship. I felt very close and totally in love.

"He began to tell me about what it was like to die; at first he was filled with rage, pain and frustration that the clerk didn't seem to understand his pleas to call an ambulance. He had been stabbed in the heart and needed help. After a short while, which felt interminable while he was experiencing it, he said he left his body and floated above it and saw the body below him, and felt detached from it, like it was just a body. He was filled with peace and love. And he felt no pain.

"After telling me this, he then said that he had to go. His feet started to move very fast, and he began to leave me behind on the path. I told him that I could do that too, and put some effort into 'powering up' my feet to make them go super fast. I actually started to rev up and move along the path quickly, and felt as if I was traveling up a tunnel of forest toward the sunlight at the top of the hill. As I began to keep pace with him, he said,

'NO!' in a very powerful voice, and I woke up in my bed, feeling hurt.

"I looked for him, to tell him about my dream. He wasn't there, and his side of the bed showed that he had not slept in the bed that night. It was dawn. I began to get irritated, thinking that he must have gone off with some friends, and feeling upset at how irresponsible he was behaving. I went to where we kept our bicycles to see if his was there and it wasn't. I was so angry that I broke the bicycle lock and chain off of my bicycle with my bare hands (he had taken both keys with him), and set off down the street toward the corner store. His bicycle was near the store, and a patrolman was standing next to it. I asked him where my husband was, and why his bicycle was sitting there. He asked my name and address, and refused to tell me anything more. He suggested that I go back home, and that someone would explain everything to me later. In about fifteen minutes a police officer and a clergyman came by and told me that Herb had been killed the night before.

"The dream braced me for this news, and although I was in shock, I felt assured constantly that he was not in his body, and a comforting presence was with me throughout the next few days of viewing the body, the funeral and other unpleasant business.

"Two days after the funeral, I was preparing for bed and contemplating suicide to join Herb, so that we could be together on the other side or in our next phase of incarnation or whatever. I consciously thought a question, 'Should I kill myself to join Herb, or stay here?'

"I then went to bed. I was just falling asleep when I felt a presence by my right side, and looked to see Herb, naked and glowing with a soft, beautiful white light. He looked beautiful *and I felt filled with love and happiness to see him. He spoke mentally to me, and said, 'This is our son,' indicating my womb, 'Take good care of him.' I had no question then about my purpose, and have tried to do the best possible job taking care of my son ever since. It did not at all seem strange that he used the word 'son', although these were the days before ultrasound and I did not know what I was having. I did give birth to a boy."*

There are many stories like this one; all indicating that there is a strong telepathic element to shared death experiences. Another such example comes from Melvin Morse, a pediatrician who has extensively studied the spiritual experiences of children. This is a shared experience that took place between a teenage boy who was struck by a truck and killed and his deaf sister. It is a brief yet beautiful story that seems to prove a telepathic experience.

"Shane, a seventeen-year-old boy, was struck by a truck and thrown through the air. He was taken to the hospital with massive head injuries. By the time his parents arrived, he had died while on life support. The parents went home to break the news to their fifteen-year-old daughter, who was deaf. When they went into the house they found her in a trance. She was talking to someone she said was her brother. She said she awoke from a nap and was able to look around the room but at the same time she seemed to be in another world. She described the accident to her parents and knew that her brother was dead, but she was also able to talk to him. 'I'm going to show you something really cool,' he said to her. He took her high above the accident scene and then, the girl said, they went to heaven. She could see her

parents standing in the living room, but could see and commu-
nicate with her brother at the same time. 'I know something you
don't know,' Shane said to his sister. He told her that their aunt
was pregnant with a boy, a fact unknown to the family at that
time. It was true."

Telepathy is a marvel, something that seems difficult to deny most of the time. We all seem to have it, don't we? It does seem likely that telepathy plays a strong role in shared death experiences, but exactly how is not completely clear.

Shared death experiencers are not ill.

Skeptics think that near-death experiences are just the brain shutting down at the point of death—no less and certainly no more. Called the "dying brain hypothesis," this theory says that all the phenomena of the near-death experience are merely hallucinations of the brain as it nears the end of its functional life.

But what if one were to have such an experience and *not* be near death? What if one had an out-of-body experience, saw deceased relatives, went up a mystical tunnel and had a life review *without* being on the verge of dying? What does it mean to be perfectly healthy and experience these things?

Those are some of the question asked of me by a man in Europe who told me of a very extensive shared death experience that he had with his mother. She was dying of breast cancer in her home in Barcelona, Spain. This man, Eduardo, was caring for his mother in her final days. His sister was with him and when they needed extra help, people from the neighborhood volunteered their time and services. "My mother was very well respected in the community," said Eduardo. "She took care of needy people through the church. She was quiet about it, but everyone knew that she devoted much time to others."

The day she died was dark and miserable, said Eduardo:

"I knew she was going to die soon and I sat on the edge of her bed to be close. To my amazement, she sat straight up and put her arms around me. Her eyes were like pearls of bright light and she was perfectly in charge of her faculties, which she had not been over the last several days.

"As I held her, a globe of bright light formed around us. If I had to put it in terms of feet, I would say that the globe was about six or seven feet wide. It completely enclosed my mother and me and I noticed that the furniture and walls and so forth in the room looked distorted, like you were seeing them through a water drop.

"Apparently my mother could tell that I wanted to ask her things about my childhood, because three-dimensional images began to fall on the globe. They were scenes from my childhood and they cleared up all of the mystery I had about this time in my life. They were too personal to reveal, but they explained me to me.

"My mother began to move away from me. It was as though she was one hundred feet down a tunnel but right with me as

well. As this took place I saw scenes of my life, including my own birth. I saw scenes from her life too, events of torment during her childhood that I had never known. I could also sense her thought process as a result of these events, and how she adapted to them and used the negative events in her life to become the kind of person she became. I could see how her attitude had trickled down into my life with purely beneficial effects on my character.

"This may sound unbelievable, but Christ was with us in the globe. I could not see the human figure of him, but I knew it was he standing in the intense light that was with us. My mother was his focus, but he spoke to me too. As a matter of fact, I had a very humorous exchange with him, one that changed the character of my relationship with God. Christ was there to help my mother with the scenes in her life and to help her understand them.

"When my mother died, I felt her body just let go and the energy go out of her. At that moment the globe we were in disappeared and I was back in the reality of this world, which I no longer consider to be reality. The world I found inside that globe was reality. For some reason, God granted me the privilege of going right to heaven's door with my mother."

Eduardo felt honored to have had this experience, and it showed. His wife, who was with him as he told me the story, said that the shared death experience had brought her husband out of his shell. In fact, people at the mother's funeral thought Eduardo had had a nervous breakdown because his morose demeanor had been replaced by a pleasant one. Still, he told no one but his wife and his sister what had happened at the deathbed of his mother.

"I am a financial planner and have worked hard to build my standing in the business world," he said. "If my business associates heard about this my name would be mud. Do you think any of them would let me handle their money?"

The shared death experience with his mother was a marvel, said Eduardo, because it opened him up to his own spiritual side, one that he had never examined until his mother's death. It also made something else clear to him—that a person can take a voyage into eternity without having to be dead.

"Look at me," he said. "I did not die, yet I had a near-death experience. That stuff you said about the dying brain hypothesis can't be true because—look at me—it happened to me and I am alive."

I certainly couldn't argue with that.

A new awakening

In 1975, the world woke up to near-death experiences. They had, most likely, taken place since the beginning of man. But with the publication of my book *Life After Life*, people all over the globe realized that these astonishing, inspiring and thought-provoking experiences were common and strikingly similar to one another. This startling new knowledge created an international sensation in that these love-filled experiences raised new hope for life after death.

An intense popular, academic and scientific debate about near-death experiences soon took shape. And that debate quickly divided people into two opposing sides—those who claimed that the experiences are evidence of life after death, and those who claimed that the experiences are hallucinations, a phenomenon tossed up by biochemical and electrical failures in the dying brain.

The findings about near-death experiences were so phenomenal that the biochemical and neuro-physiological explanations for them were almost comforting for many. They provided a cushion—a sort of breathing space—in which humanity could take stock of these mysterious experiences without owning up to their full implications. There was no need to rush into the world-changing conclusion that there is an afterlife. After all, medicine and science had made enormous strides in understanding the human body and mind. Certainly they would eventually reduce near-death experiences to a scientific equation, wouldn't they?

However, shared death experiences do not offer any such safety net. On the surface, it seems possible that near-death experiences are caused by electrochemical disarray in the brain. But shared death experiences are a different situation entirely. In these cases, someone who is present at another's death reports elements that overlap clearly and significantly with the near-death experience. Yet these people were not dying or even sick, an obvious fact that throws a major monkey wrench into the standard way of debating this highly important issue.

And to those who can't face the awesome prospect that a person's death experience can be shared? They run in another direction. They may fall back on the same tired explanations for phenomena that don't fit neatly into boxes of their own making. Or they declare shared death experiences to be "mass hypnosis" or "delusion" or an event "caused by suggestion." This, too, is patently ridiculous and beyond reason—there is no reason to invent a psychiatric category when nobody is sick.

To be frank, I am mystified by the shared death experience. There is no settled language to explain these experiences. But nonetheless they exist. It is as if the other side somehow opens up and invites us to take a closer look.

Peace in the midst of combat

A poet named Karl Skala had such an experience during World War II. Trapped in a foxhole during an artillery bombardment, a shell landed close and killed the soldier who was huddled with Skala. The blast pushed the soldier against Skala, who knew that the young man had been killed by the blast.

As the bombardment continued, Skala could feel himself being drawn into the heavens with the dead soldier, where they suddenly found themselves looking down onto the battlefield. As Skala held his friend he looked up and could see a bright light. The two soldiers moved at a rapid rate toward this light until Skala suddenly stopped and returned to his body. The blast left Skala nearly deaf for the rest of his life. It also made him far more spiritual.

Karl Skala started to write in 1943, while stationed in Russia, and his five books won many Austrian awards. He first earned recognition with the following poem, written about his experience with his fallen friend and comrade.

Would you really call this dying?
In the near light, but far away.
This light which our hope nurtures.
To the star high above
Everyone has traveled there in their mind
before your body, the mind, the spirit
belonged once to the stars
let this light shine deep in your heart, in your dreams
on
this earth.
Death is an awakening.

"Science without religion is lame. Religion without science is blind."

—ALBERT EINSTEIN

4

✧ ✧ ✧

ELEMENTS OF THE SHARED DEATH EXPERIENCE

THERE ARE MANY WAYS IN which people die, and many conditions under which a person's death can be shared. Soldiers may share a comrade's death on the battlefield, a daughter may share the death of her mother at her bedside, or a person may be with a stranger who is struck down by a speeding car and dies in a pubic place. But no matter the circumstances, elements of the shared death experience surface again and again.

This is completely understandable. Virtually all complex phenomena—whether in the physical world or in the metaphysical—are defined by a variety of elements that come together like pieces of a puzzle. Rarely does a person experience all of the elements of any phenomenon. So rather than experience all seven of the elements that I have defined in my research, a person having a shared death experience will most likely have a few of them—or perhaps even only one.

I have yet to have an individual tell me a shared death experience in which they have experienced all of the elements I have uncovered in my research. If they did have all of the elements, their experience would most likely resemble the theoretical model I have constructed below:

A woman I'll call Jane has been sitting at the bedside of her husband of thirty years, who is dying of cancer. He is no longer conscious and his attending physician says that death could take place at any time.

She has been talking to him and holding his hand for several hours when she is aware of a charge of energy that seems to pass through her. The feeling startles her, and later she describes it as feeling almost like the static shock you'd get from walking across a rug and touching a doorknob. The feeling energizes her and frightens her at the same time, because she can tell that her husband has actually died.

As she looks at her husband's face, a white mist rises and dissipates into the air above him. She later describes this as looking like cigarette smoke or the cloud of carbon dioxide that comes off of dry ice.

Suddenly the room becomes brighter and fills with a white light that contains swirling particles that stay suspended like dust in a dust storm. Jane feels very light-headed and suddenly realizes that she has left her body and is floating above her husband's hospital bed. She can see herself sitting next to his dead body, which now seems even stranger because she is also aware of him floating next to her. She looks at her husband and sees that he is smiling, which is in stark contrast to the dead man she sees below.

As the two hover together, scenes from their life spring up around them. They travel through their life in memory frag-ments, many of which have a panoramic quality to them; it's as though she is surrounded by a movie of her own life. The scenes begin with their first joyous meeting and run all the way through the difficult and tender times they had as he went into his decline and eventual death. In the midst of these memory fragments are scenes that Jane is not a part of, scenes that were a part only of her husband's life. She sees him struggling through boot camp and feels his pain as he falls from a rope that he had to climb as part of physical training. She sees him with girlfriends that he had before they met. She has a better understanding of her husband than ever before.

The couple begins to move toward the corner of the room, which is no longer a right angle. The entire room has changed shape and still seems to be in a state of flux, Jane notices. Per-haps this change is due to a tube that seems to be opening near the ceiling like a portal to elsewhere. Jane and her late husband enter it. She has the sense of moving very quickly up this tube, a sensation that lasts for a few seconds until she finds they have slowed down and are now emerging into a heavenly realm.

The landscape that surrounds Jane and her husband is stunning. She describes it later as being like a beautiful national park, except that the plants are glowing from inside, as if they each have their own internal source of light.

Jane and her husband walk together down a path. As they approach a stream, Jane suddenly becomes aware that she can go no further. Although nothing is said, she has the feeling that the stream is a barrier beyond which she cannot go. She is happy for her husband because he is now pain-free and out of his mortal body. She says good-bye and in a flash is back in her earthly body, sitting in the hospital room next to her husband's corporeal body.

Jane realizes that throughout much of the experience she had been hearing music with tones that she had never heard before. The music had been present from almost the very beginning, when she saw the mist rise from her husband's body, but now it has suddenly stopped. She listens hard but can hear only silence. She looks down at her dead husband and doesn't quite know how to feel. She thought she would be sad and depressed at his death, but now she feels strangely elated because she knows that his spirit has survived bodily death.

Still she is stunned and puzzled and wants to know, "Did that really happen?"

It is important to keep in mind that the above narrative is a hypothetical model of a full-blown shared death experience. Although the elements I have found by examining dozens of case studies are represented in it, they don't necessarily happen in the order I have presented, nor do they necessarily "go all the way" as the ones represented above. Sometimes, for example, people might be out of their body for seconds, or they may have a life review that is not as long or as complete as another person's. There is variety in all spiritual experience, yet it is clear that they are transformative almost regardless of their length. I interpret this to mean that even just a glimpse into the spiritual world is enough to bring promise that a loved one's demise is merely a shifting of their spirit to another plane.

I also want to make clear that not all who are with a loved one when they die experience any of these things. I will say with some assurance, however, that a sizeable percentage of people who are with another person as they die will describe feelings that clearly indicate they felt a part of something deeply spiritual. These experiences are often compared to witnessing a birth and are considered by many to be joyful, loving events. Here is one such example from an e-mail sent to me by a woman in Germany who cared for a friend as she took her last breath:

"Rosemary died ten days after she took to her bed and got weaker every day. On the night of her death I was holding her head and gradually her breath became more noisy and erratic. Sometimes there were pauses before she would take another breath and it sounded very difficult. It was 2:00 AM and I was tired after several days and nights of intensive caring and watching her life ebbing away, so I closed my eyes for a moment whilst her labored breathing continued. Immediately, once my eyes were shut, I saw a tunnel with an intense light at the end of it. It was very strong and clear and I was so startled that I opened my eyes again in surprise.

"I took it as a sign that Rosemary had already passed away, but just after I opened my eyes she died with a giant outbreath, pushing her head deeply into the cushion of my hands, which were still holding her but were not strong enough to resist her push. It felt to me as if she was giving birth to herself in that very moment."

Let's look at the elements that make up the shared death experience.

Change of geometry

This trait is difficult to describe because it takes so many different shapes. It is also one that is not found in near-death experiences. A woman who was at the bedside of her dying brother said it was as though the square room she was in "shifted" into another shape. As one man, a math teacher, described it, "It was as though the room collapsed and expanded at the same time. It was as though I was witnessing an alternative geometry."

For many, this change of geometry means that the room simply seems to change shape. Others have said that the room changes shape but also opens into an "alternative reality" that is described in various ways. Some say that the room opens into a world where "time is not a factor." One woman described the feeling she had as one in which "spirits could see in and look at us, but we could not see them." Another woman said "the room was like Disneyland in that it made me realize that most of the stuff that happens in the world happens behind the scenes and that all we see is the surface, where the functioning part is."

If I had to summarize all of these descriptions I would say that they are like some kind of hatch popping open at the point of death and leading to a different and larger dimension, a description that is borne out to a large extent by the experience of Nancy, whose brother was dying of congestive heart failure at a hospital in North Carolina. As she said,

"Since I didn't know how long he would last, I decided to stay in the room with him, sitting at his bedside.

"After a day or so of waiting, his breathing became more labored and then he stopped breathing altogether. I held his hand and the nurse came in and stood by the bed. He had a Do Not Resuscitate (DNR) order, but she wanted to make sure his last moments were comfortable.

"All of a sudden I felt the room change shape, almost like it filled with air and inflated. Then I felt myself lift out of my body and join my brother in midair! We literally swirled around the room as spirits and then I felt myself return to my body and the perspective I have always had. While we were flying around the room, I could see myself sitting next to my brother and I could see my brother in the air with me. When I returned to my body the room returned to its shape, which was all right angles."

As a postscript to this story, the brother did not die. His heart started again spontaneously and he lived another day. When he finally died, she did not glimpse the spiritual realm again.

Mystical light

One of the most profound elements of the near-death experience is what I call the light experience. In this element, the dying person finds himself or herself bathed in a mystical light, one that seems to have substance to it, as though it were almost liquid. One of Melvin Morse's study patients described it perfectly when she said, "I liked the light. That's where all of the good things are."

This mystical light is also present in many shared death experiences. It is described variously as a "crystalline light," one that emits "purity," "love" and "peace." Some say that the light "pulses" with these elements while at the same time having a depth and seriousness to it. This is no ordinary light, but one that increases a person's wisdom, spiritual transformation and other mystical elements. A woman described the light this way: "When Mom died, everyone present saw the room fill with light from 'an angelic presence.'" Another woman, who held her teenaged son as he died, said that "witnessing the light was like being swept up into a cloud."

A man who was with his wife as she passed said, "The room became uncomfortably bright, so bright that when I shut my eyes I couldn't shut out the light. But still it was comforting. In the light I could feel her. She had gone physically, but was still with me in spirit." He went on to say that the light was "vivid and bright, but not in the way that we see with our eyes."

Sometimes the eyes of the dying person light up, while during others, the dying person actually lights up herself, in what has been described as a translucent glow. Here is one such experience, as told by a hospice nurse in North Carolina from beginning to end so you can see how the light fits in with other elements:

"When I was a student nurse my biggest dread was seeing someone die. I had a terrible image drawn from movies and my overactive imagination. I certainly understood it came with the territory. Still, I didn't know if I was going to be able to take it when I saw a patient die. I made some flimsy excuse about going to get some equipment when it became apparent that Mrs. Jones was about to die.

"I was hightailing it out of the room when I heard a soft voice I recognized as Mrs. Jones's. It was clearly coming from inside my head yet obviously coming from her too. This voice insisted, 'Don't worry. I'm fine now.' I was drawn back into her room as though by a magnet. I saw her draw her last breath. Right then a light that looked like vapor formed over her face. I never had felt such peace. The head nurse on duty was very calm and told me that Mrs. Jones was leaving her body and that she wanted me to see the dying experience.

"I saw a luminous presence floating near the bed, shaped somewhat like a person. The head nurse saw the light in the room and this tremendous light coming from Mrs. Jones's eyes but not the presence.

"The nurse encouraged me by saying that she had witnessed similar appearances at other times. The nurse sat with me for a long time afterwards and we talked and prayed for Mrs. Jones.

"Since then I have never been uncomfortable around dying patients. I have used this experience to teach student nurses."

Many of my fellow researchers feel it is the encounter with the mystical light that leads to positive changes in the personalities of those who have a near-death experience. The research of Dr. Morse bears this out.

He examined the effects of the various elements of a near-death experience—many of them also present in shared death experiences—on those who have had them. He concluded that spiritual encounters with light are the element most profoundly linked with positive transformation. As Morse put it: "It doesn't matter who has the experience—Marines, punk rockers, real-estate agents, corporate executives, housewives, ministers or holy men—they are all transformed by their exposure to the light."

The experience of the light has no known origin in the brain. Numerous scientific researchers have documented that every element of the near-death experience—being out-of-body, traveling up the tunnel, seeing dead relatives, having a life review, seeing visions of heaven—can be found to reside in various parts of the brain, yet none of the reductionist researchers has yet been able to find the anatomical origin of the mystical light.

It is too early to tell if the experience of light is as transformative for those who have shared death experiences, but further study will certainly reveal the answer to that and other questions. Based on the stories I have heard, however, I suspect that the light will be found to transform those who share in another's death too. Virtually everyone I have spoken to who has seen the light in a shared death situation talks about its positive effects, both when they first saw it and even years later. Perhaps it is just the memory of the light or it is a physical or spiritual change that is long-lasting. Whatever the case, many people respond to the light in the way that Sharon Nelson of Maryland did. She told me of her brush with the light at the deathbed of her sister and its long-term effects:

"About ten years ago, my very beloved sister was dying of cancer at home in her bedroom. I was present along with my other sister and my brother-in-law. About one week prior to my sister's actual passing, a bright white light engulfed the room. It was a light that we all saw and a light that has stayed with us ever since. I felt an intense love and connection with everyone in the room, including other 'souls' that were not visible but that we felt the presence of.

"For me, I saw nothing except this white light and my ill sister. For many years I thought that this light said to me, 'This house, these things, they are not real.' I was confused about why those thoughts had come to my mind, but I now realize I was experiencing what my dying sister was experiencing. What a revelation! Words cannot express what impact this experience had on me. This was certainly not something I had ever thought before. The wisdom and peace of this light have not left me since."

Another case study that makes me think the light has a long-lasting effect on those who witness it came to me during a medical conference in Spain. I was there talking about near-death studies and asked the audience if anyone had personal knowledge of shared death experiences.

At the end of my talk, two sisters approached me and told of being present at the death of their father. He was dying of cancer, said the sister named Louisa, and hadn't responded for several days. The two didn't dare leave the hospital room, fearing they would not be in attendance when he finally passed over. Finally, they noticed that his breathing had become extremely sporadic, so much so that there were several times they thought he had passed away.

It was during one of these breathless periods that a "brilliant light" filled the room. The sisters became both frightened and hopeful, since the bright light also caused their father to stir slightly. A few minutes later, though, their father stopped breathing and died.

"The light stayed for maybe ten minutes after he died," said Maria, the other sister. "We saw no forms or figures in the light, but it seemed to be alive and have a personal presence."

It was this personal presence that made them think that the light consisted of their father's "essence," said the sisters. And yes, they felt changed for the better by the light.

Stories like the two above make me think that exposure to this light and all the "good things" that are in it has a long-term effect. More research is necessary to know if that is true.

Music and musical sounds

A frequent perception in a shared death experience is the sound of music. Sometimes both the person dying and a bystander report the sounds. At other times, many people hear the music.

There are several examples of this musical phenomenon at the point of death. This one comes from a woman I interviewed in Maryland who heard music at the bedside of her dying husband. She tells her story:

"He was in a coma and on a respirator but I had no idea the end was coming so soon. I spent the night in the room with him and he passed away at 5:30 AM. I was awake and his parents had just come in.

"I sat in the corner in a chair. I was exhausted. Suddenly I became aware of a lot of people around the bed. I could see the entire room as if it was on a stage. People were gathering around. I could see him in the bed and suddenly it was like glitter was coming down from the corner of the room. Along with this I heard music.

"I asked everyone to be quiet so I could listen to the music. As the music got louder the glitter became heavier and moved over to my husband.

"This was the most beautiful and intricate music I had ever heard. Every note was a piece of glitter. I was seeing music. There were billions of notes and it reminded me of the feeling I get in church when I hear handbells. It was very beautiful and very intricate.

"In the middle of this, the nurse came over and touched me on the arm and told me that my husband was dead. He died when the glitter touched him."

Here is another example, this from the nineteenth-century researchers Edmund Gurney, Frederic W.H. Myers and Frank Podmore. They interviewed the family of a girl named Lilly, all of whom heard music for several days before and after her death. Her father described the music filling the room as "the soft, wild notes of an Aeolian harp." Lilly's mother reported, "My old nurse and aunt came up to see how Lilly was, and were with my husband, all in the room with the child. I had gone down into the kitchen ... when the same sounds of Aeolian music were heard by all three in the room, and I heard the same music in the kitchen."

Out-of-body experience

An out-of-body event is a fairly common element of a shared death experience. During this phenomenon, a person has a strong sense that they have moved to a position from which they can observe their own physical body and all that is around it.

A shared death experience frequently begins with the subject feeling a surge of unnatural energy or hearing a rushing sound. Then the subject finds himself suddenly looking at the physical scene below from a distant perspective, usually one near the ceiling or in an upper corner of the room. From that viewpoint they are able to watch their interaction with the person who is dying.

A typical example of the out-of-body experience is one told to me by a forty-four-year-old woman from Carrollton, Georgia, who told me about the surge of energy she felt when her father died in her arms. She heard a rushing sound that became very high-pitched, "like a jet engine revving up." Then, she says, "I floated out of my body and could see myself leaning forward and looking puzzled at Dad as he died. I could see myself holding his hand and smiling. Mixed in with this, I could see vivid images of my childhood as he sort of narrated them like they were old family movies. The light became very bright and then went away and I was back in my body, holding my father's hand."

Sometimes, the subject is not alone in their out-of-body experience. Rather, they are with the spiritual body of the deceased person. Often, the person who has died looks much younger in their spiritual body, and usually much happier. The subject has the sense that the deceased was pleased to have shed his or her physical body and is looking forward to the next stage of existence.

One such example came to me from a woman in Charlottesville, Virginia, who was introduced to me by a fellow doctor who didn't quite know how to address the issues being discussed with him. Dana, a vivacious fortysomething patient, said she had had some kind of near-death experience when her husband died.

Dana's husband, Jim, had been diagnosed with pancreatic cancer and was dying rapidly. He wanted to die at home, he said, but soon realized that he needed hospital care so he would not be a burden to his wife. He checked in to the Martha Jefferson Hospital and within a few days was in a coma. I'll let Dana tell the rest of the story:

"The night Jim died, I was sitting next to him, holding his hand, when we both left our bodies and began to fly through the air! It was amazing, frightening and puzzling. We left the hospital room and began to swoop over the city. As we did this, beautiful music like I've never before heard started to play. It was like dance music, but it was completely unique in that I've never heard anything like it since then. As the music became higher in pitch, we began to climb higher above the city. Above us was a bright light, and we were headed directly for it. The light was

beautiful and vibrant and powerful. I felt comfort and joy being close to it and Jim was smiling and staring directly at it. The last I saw of him, he was smiling very broadly."

Dana said that she was sucked back into her body, where she found out what she already knew—that her husband had died.

This experience took the edge off the loss of Dana's husband. "I went partway to heaven with Jim," Dana said. "I know where he went."

These shared out-of-body experiences are always uncanny, but some are more so than others. For example, after a lecture to doctors at Fort Dix, the U.S. Army base in New Jersey, a sergeant approached me and told about a remarkable experience that I later confirmed with his attending physicians:

"I was terribly ill and near death with heart problems at the same time that my sister was near death with a diabetic coma in another part of the same hospital. I left my body and went into the corner of the room, where I watched them work on me down below.

"Suddenly, I found myself in conversation with my sister, who was up there with me. I was very attached to her, and we were having a great conversation about what was going on down there when she began to move away from me.

"I tried to go with her but she kept telling me to stay where I was. 'It's not your time,' she said. 'You can't go with me because it's not your time.' Then she just began to recede off into the distance through a tunnel while I was left there alone.

"When I awoke, I told the doctor that my sister had died. He denied it, but at my insistence, he had a nurse check on it. She had in fact died, just as I knew she did."

Although no one yet knows how often out-of-body experiences occur among those who have shared death experiences, they are among the most common events to take place during a near-death experience. More than 75 percent of near-death experiencers surveyed in a study done by Jeffrey Long, MD, of the Near Death Experience Research Foundation (NDERF) answered "yes" when asked the question, "Did you experience a separation of your consciousness from your body?" during their close brush with death.

Co-living a life review

An amazing component of many shared death experiences is what I call the "co-living" of a life review. The life review involves an intense review of the one's earthly life. It may be a panoramic view of the individual's entire life, or just significant fragments. In a recent study by NDERF, almost 23 percent of near-death experiencers surveyed reported having had a life review. These are typical life reviews:

"I saw my life flash before me shortly after I left my body and was still in the hospital room. I was told that I was going to

help educate and teach many people and that is exactly what I am doing now."   —Steve, 62, cardiac-arrest patient

"I saw all my flaws and where I had been going wrong in my life, as well as my good points."   —Jenna, 56, automobile accident

"I saw every important event that had ever happened in my life, from my first birthday to my first kiss, to fights with my parents. I saw how selfish I was and how I would give anything to go back and change."   —Donna, 19, attempted suicide

The shared, or "co-lived," life review is different from the ones that take place in the near-death experience. For one thing, the person having it is not near death, but is sharing the life review of the person who is dying. This description of a shared life review sums it up perfectly: "I was standing in front of what felt like a large screen with my husband who had just died as we watched his life unfold before us. Some of what I saw I had not known before."

A woman from San Diego told me about being at the bedside of her teenage son, who was dying of complications from diabetes. When he finally died, she saw all of the scenes of his life around them, as if she were standing in the midst of real events happening very quickly. I will let her tell her entire story so you can see for yourself how the life review fits in with other events in this remarkable shared experience:

"When my fifteen-year-old son died I was there in the room with him. He had diabetes from a very young age and, of course,

that greatly complicated his life. Because of the dependence that diabetes creates, my son and I were exceptionally close.

"*I was holding his hand when he died and I felt the life force surge from him, somewhat like an electric current, although vibration might be a more appropriate term. The shape of the room changed all at once and instead of the hospital room there was a field of intense light far and away brighter than anything anyone can imagine who has not seen it for themselves. In place of the hospital room and the medical equipment a vision appeared of everything my son had ever done in his brief life. He was there right in the middle of it, beaming a bright smile of joy.*

"*I know that this is inconceivable for others, but as sad as I was to lose him, I felt the joy of his release from the constant discomfort and concern of the diabetes. It was just his time, is the best way I can describe what I understood at that moment.*

"*I saw Christ swoop in and lift him out of his body—I really did. I saw my son leave his body and enter into this intense, bright light in which he and I were surrounded by scenes of his life, down to the smallest details. I saw many things I had long since forgotten and also many things I had never known about at all. I saw him alone in his room playing with his Fort Apache set for example, and talking on the phone with his friends when he was a teenager.*

"*The light that surrounded and illuminated his life was Christ—that much I know. But personally I didn't have the feeling that Christ cared whether anyone called him by that name or not, only that they know the love that was present and fills us all regardless of whether we realize it.*

"*You could say that the scenes from his life were flashes, or almost electric discharges, utterly indescribable. I was forty years old at that time, but since then I have felt a hundred years old even though I am only sixty-two. I do not mean that negatively, by the way. By saying I feel a hundred I mean in terms of wisdom. Socrates said wisdom means knowing what you don't know and that is how I feel, exactly.*

"Parts of my son's life and our interaction were blurred out, like the views you see on TV when they are trying to conceal someone's face. There was no feeling that anything bad was being concealed, however, only that this was not the occasion for it to surface.

"I feel there is a lot more to this that I will grasp fully when I die and meet my son again. In the meantime, it is my duty to stay here and live this life serving others while hopelessly trying to puzzle it out."

Another extraordinary example of a co-lived life review came to me from a student at the University of Virginia. I was going to a basketball game with my sons when a young man approached and asked if he could speak to me. He had recognized me from an article in the newspaper and wanted to tell me about an incident that happened when his twin brother died.

The two were very close, he said, in that way that only twins can be. Over the course of their lives they'd had several incidents take place that could best be described as psychic. But what happened when his brother died surpassed any explanation he could come up with. Here is what he told me:

"My brother and I are identical twins and have always felt linked. We did things like call our parents at the same time from

different locations, and more than once we selected the same card for our mother on her birthday or at Mother's Day. Sometimes we even sensed when something had happened to the other, whether it was good or bad. We were very close.

"One weekend my brother went to another state for a high-school football game and I stayed here at home. He drove there with friends, and on the day he was returning, I was lying on the couch watching sports when I suddenly had the sensation of leaving my body and moving toward a bright light. As this happened I flashed back on events that had taken place with my brother. I relived several events from our childhood, including some things that were so insignificant that I had forgotten them. These were all memory images, but none of them were daydreams or the same as sleeping dreams. They were so vivid that I really thought I was reliving them."

The young man had no idea how long the episode lasted, but when it was over he found himself back in his body and deeply disturbed. He immediately told his mother what had taken place and sat up on the couch trying to relax. About an hour later, he said, his mother received a telephone call from the police in the other state that her son had been killed in an automobile accident.

Another case study involving a co-lived life review came from a man named Ted, who was introduced to me by a fellow doctor. A career railroad worker, Ted was at the deathbed of a friend who was suffering from lung cancer. The two men had worked together on the railroad for nearly twenty years and—as Ted told me—"I wanted to be with him when he made his final stop."

As the friend labored to breathe, Ted sat with his hand on his shoulder. The friend's breathing slowed and then finally stopped. Ted said he could tell when his friend died because a wispy, transparent "something"—as formless as smoke—came up from his chest. What he saw shocked him, and then the surprises continued:

"All of a sudden I was above my body, watching the scene below. I could feel movement, like the kind you feel when a train leaves the station and the ground shifts, or you are on one train and another next to you starts moving.

"The room around us became very bright and then I started to see flashes—scenes—of all the years we had worked together on the rails."

I asked Ted for some specifics of the life review and he thought a moment.

"One of the events really stood out. We were checking the boxcars one night in Illinois. It was a very cold night, so bitter cold that I had sweaters and a down jacket on and a wool cap and thick gloves and I could still hardly stand to be outside.

"As we walked down the line of cars, we found a drunk drifter lying in the grass next to the train. He was not dressed very warm and wasn't responding very well to us, even though we were shaking him pretty hard to wake him up. He was obviously drunk, but also was having a problem with hypothermia. The engineer was radioing us to hurry up, but when we found that drunk we called the local police and told the engineer that

we had to wait with the man until the police came to make sure he didn't freeze to death."

As Ted relived this event with me, what came back to him was the importance of compassion over expediency. "The engineer was mad as heck that we didn't just let the guy go, but if we had he would have died."

It was obviously a memory that affected the man deeply. He teared up as he talked about witnessing the event again. "I'm glad we took care of that man," he said. "Everyone wanted us to leave him, but we wouldn't do it. He would have frozen to death."

Encountering unworldly or "heavenly" realms

Visiting a heavenly realm is one of the most common elements of a near-death experience. In recent studies of this phenomenon, more than 50 percent of people who have had a near-death experience say they entered a heavenly realm or an unearthly location during their episode. When pressed for descriptions of what they saw, their answers are surprisingly similar. Here are several accounts from people who have had near-death experiences so you can see how they compare to those from shared death experiences:

"I was walking through a very bright tunnel, and walking very confidently even though I could see nothing but light, not even where my feet were landing. Then I came out of

the light and onto a hillside where the landscape was perfect and the mountains were rolling and soft. There was nothing but blue sky and green hills and big trees in the distance. It gave me a feeling like no other place I have ever been."
—A man who had a heart attack while walking in New York City

"There were perfect plants and colors that were indescribable—greens, reds, blues—all of the colors that are around us every day except they were so perfect that the colors I see now seem dull. But beyond the view was the music! The music was like nothing I have ever heard. It was clear and deep and came to me through some other way besides my ears."
—A woman who was struck by a car

"I climbed a big hill and at the top I could see a city off in the distance. The air was so clear that I thought I was looking at a pile of diamonds until I realized it was the lights of the city and I was looking at their sparkle."
—A child who nearly drowned

When people who have had a near-death experience discuss the heavenly realm, they frequently use words like "paradise," "pure," "serene" and "heavenly" in their descriptions. The same is true of those who have shared death experiences.

Here is one such example from a doctor in Maine who told me a story about two friends, Martha and Katherine. Martha was in the hospital with a failing heart that had become enlarged and was close to stopping. The doctor told her as carefully as he could that she could die at any moment. He was surprised at the old Mainer's response. "I don't mind dying. I'm ready—I just want to go fast."

Katherine, a friend of Martha's, came to stay with her at the hospital. When it became obvious that Martha was close to death, Katherine got into bed with her and hugged her friend close as she waited to die. And before long, Martha's heart did give out. Katherine said she felt a jolt of energy as her friend died, and she responded reflexively by squeezing her friend's chest, which restarted her heart. Her efforts were successful and soon Martha was back to life and angry with Katherine.

"I'm ready to go," she barked. "Get out of bed and don't try to start my heart again."

Katherine crawled out and sat on a chair next to the bed. She promised Martha that next time her heart stopped, she would not attempt any heroic measures.

Within an hour, Katherine noticed that Martha's breathing had become labored. As she listened longer, she noticed that Martha had nearly stopped breathing. As Katherine listened even more closely, she began to hear a buzzing in her own ear, which grew louder and louder. Then, Katherine told the doctor, she was no longer in her own body:

"I was suddenly walking up a hill with Martha and we were surrounded by light. Not an ordinary light, but everything around us—plants, the ground, even the sky, glowed with its own light. It was unbelievably beautiful. I am sure this place was heaven or some place like it, because there was a feeling that was wonderful. I honestly felt fifty years younger!

"Ahead of us I could see her dead husband and other deceased relatives, and they were all coming down this hill to meet her. The terrain and plants of the hill were wonderful. Everything was shockingly green and carried a glow that I couldn't keep my eyes off of. Martha was moving quite nicely up the hill and soon she gave me a push on the arm that meant to me that I should stop, and I did. I always did what Martha told me to do and figured I shouldn't stop now. Then the buzzing in my ears stopped and I felt myself return to my body right here at the hospital."

Also present in this heavenly realm is a border beyond which the living person cannot follow the one who is dying. The gentle touch on the arm by Martha in the above story is an example of this barrier. Martha was clearly indicating to her friend that she should go no farther in their journey.

The border seen in both near-death and shared death experiences is usually something like a bridge, river or plant, or—as in Katherine's experience—a nudge from the deceased, and it is generally interpreted as a boundary from beyond which the subject will not return.

Although there is no data regarding the number of times people with shared death experiences encounter a border, the current largest study on near-death experiencers—NDERF's examination of more than thirteen hundred case studies—estimates that more than 30 percent of people who die and then come back to life "reach a boundary or physically limiting structure" during the experience. And as with near-death experiencers, those who share the death experience are not always happy to return. Said one of the people surveyed: "It was blissful to leave my body and go with dad. But when I came back it was like—slam!—I was back in my body and feeling cheated because I couldn't have gone further."

Mist at death

Since I first began to study death, I have heard people tell of a mist that is emitted from the body of those who die. Those who are attending the deathbed usually see this mist. They describe it in various ways. Some say that it looks like white smoke, while others say it is as subtle as steam. Sometimes it seems to have a human shape. Whatever the case, it usually drifts upward and always disappears fairly quickly.

Here is one such example from a doctor in Georgia. In this account, he describes events in which he saw mist being emitted from patients at two separate times. I am including his description of both experiences so you can see the mist experience in its context:

"I have seen mist coming up from deceased patients twice in a six-month period. As the patients died they lit up with a bright glow—eyes shining with a silvery light. A mist formed over the chest area and hovered there.

"Time stood still for me as I watched this happen. I watched very closely, focusing as intently as I could. The mist had depth and complex structure. It seemed to have layers with energetic

motion in it, which is a poor description, I know, but just think of something as subtle as water moving within water.

"During the second occurrence, I felt an unseen presence, as though someone was standing beside me and waiting for the patient to die. I have no idea who or what the presence was, but if I had to guess I would say that it was someone who loved the patient. That is the feeling I got."

A few days after the second experience, this doctor had a spontaneous out-of-body experience. To me this implies that he was primed to have such an experience by what had happened at the deathbeds of these two patients. This experience, too, profoundly affected the physician's view of the world. As he said, "I was trying to get to sleep when I was suddenly looking at my own body in the bed below. Between seeing the mist rise from two patients and my own out-of-body experience, I can say with assurance that there is more to the world than there seems."

Another description of the mist that arises during death comes from a hospice psychologist in North Carolina, who includes it with a number of other phenomena associated with shared death experiences:

"The deathbed scene is not fully in this world. And although I am not religious, hospice work has awakened me to a spiritual dimension of life.

"In my opinion, everyone who works with the dying long enough must have some awareness of these experiences. I believe the spiritual experiences of dying people somehow leak out and pervade the area around them. If you step into that area with the right temperament, you will receive, I feel, a sense of the sacred in the presence of the dying.

"I have experienced the room taking on a different configura-tion a number of times. The only way that I can describe it is that moving energy pulses through the room. I often feel something that I can't name.

"The bedside of the dying offers a view into eternity. Like looking through a window into elsewhere, from time to time I see lights and twice have had clear views of what appear to be structures. On both occasions I saw patients leave their bodies in a cloud form. I saw them rise out of their bodies and head toward these structures.

"I would describe these clouds as a sort of mist that forms around the head or chest. There seems to be some kind of elec-tricity to it, like an electrical disturbance. I don't know if I see it with my physical eyes, but it's there all the same.

"There is no doubt in my mind that you can sometimes see people depart for the other side."

Here is yet another example, this from the research of Robert Crookall, published in a 1967 collection of case studies entitled *Events on the Threshold of the Afterlife*: "I ap-proached the ward as the child drew its final breath. Then I saw mist above the little body. It took the shape of the body that lay on the bed. This was attached by a fine sil-ver cord. The replica was about three feet from the body on the bed. It rose gradually to above five feet above the body, and then gradually lifted itself into an upright posi-tion. It then floated away."

I don't know how to interpret the mist that some see at the point of death. It makes no sense to think of it as a hallucination, especially given that those who have seen it report that it appears just as the loved one dies. It makes little sense that it would always appear at the same time in the dying process if it were a hallucination.

"A different world"

The seven elements above identify the shared death experience, but I have yet to find a person who reports all seven. Likewise, no case study includes just one element. Usually, a person reports several of the seven elements in their experience.

One very common trait of the shared death experience is ineffability. Nearly everyone who contributed their story to my study says that the experience is very difficult to explain in words. One person described it thusly:

"It's like going to a different world. When our men went to the moon, they could describe the physical landscape right away, but it took a while to process the mystical landscape and how this new world affected them spiritually. That's how this experience was for me. I can now tell you what happened, but its spiritual effect seems to know no bounds."

"You have to know the past to understand the present."

—DR. CARL SAGAN

5

✧✧✧

HISTORIC PARALLELS

ALTHOUGH SHARED DEATH EXPERIENCES have likely been in existence since the beginning of man, they have never been studied in an organized fashion. Rather, they have been included as a category in a form of experience known as the "deathbed vision."

In the most common form of deathbed vision, the person who is dying will see and even communicate with angelic beings or deceased relatives who have come to comfort them. There are several types of deathbed visions. Sometimes the visitor can be seen and not heard, while during others the dying person is able to speak to the visitor and receive spoken answers. Sometimes the visitor appears for only a few moments, while at other times for days. Sometimes the visitor accompanies the dying person to a heavenly plane, which they later describe to their loved ones. Still, the visions are visible only to the person who is dying. The only thing bystanders can witness is the reaction and the one side of the conversation that emanates from the loved one who is dying.

This is the most common form of deathbed vision.

Shared death experiences, as we now know, are deathbed visions that can be witnessed by bystanders as well as the person who is dying. This type of experience has always been lumped into the general category of deathbed vision, even though it is very different from the one-sided visions that are most prominent.

Curious explorers

To my knowledge, the first to research deathbed visions were Gurney, Myers and Podmore, all members of the Society for Psychical Research (SPR) in England. These three college professors were among the most active of the paranormal researchers who sprang up in England in the late nineteenth century.

This was a period of great curiosity about paranormal experiences and the afterlife. These three pioneers believed that questions about the afterlife and the paranormal could be answered with careful observation. The SPR was founded in 1882 to explore psychic and "spiritualistic" events, and, as was written in the society's first proceedings, to do so "in the same spirit of exact and unimpassioned enquiry which has enabled Science to solve so many problems."

The goal of collecting and investigating data was accomplished by these three scholars with the publication of *Phantasms of the Living,* a work designed "to lay the foundation stone of a study which will loom large in the approaching age."

The book contains more than seven hundred analyzed cases regarding a number of supernatural phenomena, including deathbed visions. It is within this body of deathbed visions that a number of excellent and puzzling shared death experiences can be found.

For example, here is one account, written by a young woman named Jeanie Gwynne-Bettany to the members of the SPR after she witnessed her mother in physical distress as she lay dying at home after collapsing from an unidentified illness:

"On one occasion (I am unable to fix the date, but I must have been about ten years old) I was walking in a country lane at A., the place where my parents then resided. I was reading geometry as I walked along, a subject little likely to produce fancies or morbid phenomena of any kind, when, in a moment, I saw a bedroom known as the White Room in my home, and upon the floor lay my mother, to all appearance dead. The vision must have remained some minutes, during which time my real surroundings appeared to pale and die out; but as the vision faded, actual surroundings came back, at first dimly, and then clearly.

"I could not doubt that what I had seen was real, so, instead of going home, I went at once to the house of our medical man and found him at home. He at once set out with me for my home,

on the way putting questions I could not answer, as my mother was to all appearance well when I left home.

"I led the doctor straight to the White Room, where we found my mother actually lying as in my vision. This was true even to minute details. She had been seized suddenly by an attack at the heart, and would soon have breathed her last but for the doctor's timely advent. I shall get my father and mother to read this and sign it."

I consider this a shared death experience because the mother was dying when her daughter had this vision.

Other examples of shared death experiences from the work of these SPR researchers are auditory experiences, ones that come from a loved one in distress (most often a long distance away) and can be heard by the percipient.

One such example came from a woman who wanted to remain anonymous, but was considered by the researchers to be "a person of thorough good sense, and with no appetite for marvels":

"On the morning of October 27, 1879, being in perfect health and having been awake for some considerable time, I heard myself called by my Christian name by an anxious and suffering voice, several times in succession. I recognised the voice as that of an old friend, almost playfellow, but who had not been in my thoughts for many weeks, or even months. I knew he was with his regiment in India, but not that he had been ordered to the front, and nothing had recalled him to my recollection.

"Within a few days I heard of his death from cholera on the morning I seemed to hear his call. The impression was so strong I noted the date and fact in my diary before breakfast."

A collective experience of vision and mist

Among the most fascinating shared death experiences to be found in this intriguing body of research was a case that the researchers called "collective," which means more than one person participated in it. As you will see, not only did two people have the experience, but they were also greatly separated. Notice also the appearance of a "misty vapour" for both percipients:

"The ... instance occurred when I was in Shanghai. It was the month of May, 1854. The night was very warm, and I was in bed, lying on my back, wide-awake, contemplating the dangers by which we were then surrounded from a threatened attack by the Chinese. I gradually became aware there was something in the room; it appeared like a thin white fog, a misty vapour, hanging about the foot of the bed. Fancying it was merely the effect of a moonbeam, I took but little notice, but after a few moments I plainly distinguished a figure that I recognized as that of my sister Fanny.

"At first the expression of her face was sad, but it changed to a sweet smile, and she bent her head toward me as if she recognized me. I was too much fascinated with the appearance to speak, although it did not cause me the slightest fear. The vision seemed to disappear gradually in the same manner as it came.

We afterward learned that on the same day my sister died—almost suddenly. I immediately wrote a full description of what I had seen to my sister, Mrs. Elmslie (the wife of the Consul at Canton) but before it reached her, I had received a letter from her, giving me an almost similar description of what she had seen the same night, adding, 'I am sure dear Fanny is gone.'

"When I promised that I would send you these particulars I at once wrote to my sister, Mrs. Elmslie, and she replied, 'I do not think I was awake when Fanny appeared to me, but I immediately awoke and saw her as you describe. I stretched out my arms to her and cried, "Fanny! Fanny!" She smiled upon me, as if sorry to leave, then suddenly disappeared.'

"When this occurred, we [i.e., Mr. de Guerin and Mrs. Elmslie] were upwards of one thousand miles apart, and neither of us had a thought of her being seriously, much less dangerously ill. Before her death she had spoken of us both to those around her bedside. She died in Jersey, on the 30th May 1854 between ten and eleven at night."

In analyzing the cases found in their work, the three researchers found that a large number of apparitional events take place close to the time of death or "some serious crisis" in the life of the person "whose presence it suggested."

The three researchers toyed with many theories to explain these deathbed visions. At one point they theorized that events like shared death experiences (although they never used the phrase) were the result of a "telepathic infection"; that our bodies contain a "meta-organism" of identical shape and structure that is "capable sometimes of detaching itself from the solid flesh and producing mea-surable effects on the material world." Another notion that the three considered was that of "superconsciousness," mental operations that rate "above the upper horizon" of consciousness.

At one point they made their strongest pronounce-ment of all: that metaphysical experiences certainly hap-pen, but "we have not at present any inkling whatever" how. "We must remember that these phantasms do not occur to please us, or to satisfy our expectations," wrote Meyers. "But rather (so far as we can tell) in accordance with some law affecting the psychical energies of the dy-ing person."

A study of deathbed visions

On the night of January 12, 1924, Dr. Florence Barrett wit-nessed what could be described as a predictive shared death experience. The obstetrical surgeon had been called into the operating room of Mother's Hospital, near Dublin, Ireland, to help deliver a child for a patient named Doris. The child appeared to be healthy, but Doris was suffering heart failure. Dr. Barrett had been called in to help attend to this emergency.

The child was delivered and still Doris' heart contin-ued to fail. Before long, the doctors realized there was little they could do to help this patient. Hoping her heart would gain strength on its own, Dr. Barrett stood at the patient's side and provided as much comfort as she could.

As Doris began to slip away, she reported seeing things. Dr. Barrett said the young woman looked eagerly toward a part of the room and as she did, a large smile crossed her face.

"Oh, lovely, lovely," she said.

"What is lovely?" asked Dr. Barrett.

"What I see," said Doris. "Lovely brightness—wonderful beings."

Dr. Barrett was later frustrated when trying to describe the young woman's depth of focus on the vision in the corner. She was totally absorbed by what she saw, and seemed to ignore her own dire condition. Then suddenly, with an almost joyous cry, the young woman exclaimed, "Why, it's Father! Oh, he is so glad I'm coming; he is so glad. It would be perfect if only W. [her husband] would come too."

The young woman's baby was brought for her to see. She looked at it with interest and then said, "Do you think I ought to stay for the baby's sake?" The question was asked to the doctors in attendance, but Doris didn't wait for their answers. Rather, she looked back at the vision and said, "I can't—I can't stay. If you could see what I do, you would know I can't stay."

The story told so far is gripping, but not one that would necessarily stand up against skeptics, who would call these visions "hallucinations," and would say that they were brought on by delirium. But the rest of the story made everyone who heard it stop and ponder eternity. Vida, the sister of Doris, had died three weeks earlier. Since Doris was in such a delicate state, her sister's death was kept from her, which is what made this deathbed story a *predictive* event, one in which another's death was revealed through the shared death experience.

As Doris lay dying, she spoke to her father, saying, "I am coming." Then, with a puzzled look on her face, said, "He has Vida with him. Vida is with him!"

When she went home that night, an exhausted Dr. Barrett told her husband what had transpired in the operating room. Sir William Barrett, a physics professor at the Royal College of Science in Dublin, was intrigued and inspired by what he heard from his wife. It was her story that led him to collect and study dozens of deathbed experiences. All of this led him to conduct the first-ever scientific study of the minds of the dying, which led him to conclude that while such patients are often clear and rational, the events around them are often spiritual and supernatural.

Barrett later produced a book of these deathbed visions entitled *Death-Bed Visions: The Psychical Experiences of the Dying.* Among the case studies presented in this book are a number of shared death experiences in which medical personnel and relatives share dying patients' visions.

Let me present a few of the case studies from Barrett's research so you can get a feel for shared death experiences from the early part of the twentieth century.

This first case comes from the editor of a journal published in England for the Society for Psychical Research. This woman told the editor the story in person. The editor found it so interesting she requested that the woman repeat the story in a letter, which she willingly did on the promise that nothing more than her initials would be published. Here, in eloquent post-Victorian language, is what she wrote:

"*Dear Madam,*

"*With reference to the incident I related to you, which happened several years ago, the following are the facts just as they occurred:*

"*I lost my daughter when she was seventeen years of age; she had been ill for some five years, and for eight months before her death had been confined to her bed. During all this time, and up to her death, she maintained a remarkable degree of intelligence and will.*

"*A fortnight before her death, one evening when I was leaning over the head of her bed, I asked her what she was thinking of, seeing her absorbed. She replied, 'Little mother, look there,' pointing to the bed-curtains. I followed the direction of her hand and saw a man's form, completely white, standing out quite clearly against the dark curtain. Having no ideas of spiritism, my emotion was intense, and I closed my eyes not wishing to see any longer. My child said to me, 'You do not reply.' I had the weakness to declare to her, 'I see nothing'; but my trembling voice betrayed me doubtless, for the child added with an air of reproach, 'Oh, little mother, I have seen the same thing for the last three days at the same hour; it's my dear father who has come to fetch me.'*

"*My child died fifteen days later, but the apparition was not repeated; perhaps it attained its greatest intensity on the day I saw it.*

"*(Signed) Z. G.*"

Here is another example from Barrett's work of what he called "collective hallucination," which he defined as "a vision seen by the relatives of the dying person as well as by the dying person herself."

In this case the narrator, Miss Emma Pearson, writes an account of her aunt's illness and death:

"My aunt, Miss Harriet Pearson, who was taken very ill at Brighton in November 1864, craved to be back in her own home in London, where she and her sister Ann (who had died some years previously) had spent practically all their lives. I accordingly made the necessary arrangements, and had her moved home. Her two nieces (Mrs. Coppinger and Mrs. John Pearson), Eliza Quinton the housekeeper, and myself did the nursing between us. She became worse and worse. On the night of December 23, Mrs. John Pearson was sitting up with her, while Mrs. Coppinger and I lay down in the adjoining room, leaving the door ajar to hear any sound from the next room. We were neither of us asleep, and suddenly we both started up in bed, as we saw someone pass the door, wrapped up in an old shawl, having a wig with three curls each side, and an old black cap. Mrs. Coppinger called to me, 'Emma, get up, it is old Aunt Ann!' I said, 'So it is; then Aunt Harriet will die today!' As we jumped up, Mrs. John Pearson came rushing out of Aunt Harriet's room, saying, 'That was old Aunt Ann. Where has she gone?' I said to soothe her, 'Perhaps it was Eliza come down to see how her old mistress is.' Mrs. Coppinger ran upstairs and found Eliza asleep. Every room was searched—no one was there; and from that day to this no explanation has ever been given of this appearance, except that it was old Aunt Ann come to call her sister. Aunt Harriet died at six that day."

Both saw the apparition

W. C. Crosby, a professor and member of the Society for Psychical Research, told another shared death experience to Barrett. A nurse saw this vision, declared Crosby, as the patient she was caring for lay unconscious on the hospital bed. The "phantom," as Barrett called the ghostly visitor, was unknown to the nurse. I want to include the story as told by Professor Crosby so you can see the detail in his investigation of this event. Here is the story:

"Mrs. Caroline Rogers, seventy-two years old, a widow who had been twice married, and whose first husband, a Mr. Tisdale, died about thirty-five years ago, has lived on Ashland Street, in Roslindale, Massachusetts, for the last twenty-five years; and since the death of her last child some years ago she has lived quite alone. Early in March of this year she was stricken with paralysis, and after an illness of nearly six weeks died on the afternoon of Tuesday, April 15.

"Mrs. Mary Wilson, a professional nurse, forty-five years old, attended Mrs. Rogers during her illness, remaining with her almost constantly until she died. She had never seen Mrs. Rogers before the latter's illness, and knew nothing of her family or history. Mrs. Rogers spoke frequently to Mrs. Wilson, and also to others, as had long been her custom, of her second husband, Mr. Rogers, and children, expressing a desire to see them again, etc.

"On the afternoon of April 14, Mrs. Rogers became unconscious, and remained so all the time until her death twenty-four hours later. Mrs. Wilson sat up with her through the whole of Monday night. Mrs. Wilson's daughter Ida, twenty-five-years-old, kept her mother company, and a boy of ten or twelve years slept in an adjoining chamber, to be called in case of an emergency. These four were the only persons in the house. The outer doors were securely locked, the door leading from the sick chamber on the second floor into the hall was kept locked all the time because it was near the foot of Mrs. Rogers' bed; and entrance to the sick chamber was gained by passing from the upper hall into the living-room by a door which was locked that night, and thence through the chamber in which the boy slept—the two chambers having been made to communicate by cutting a door through the back of a small closet. This door was diagonally facing the bed on which Mrs. Rogers lay. Mrs. Wilson rested on a settee placed at right angles to the head of Mrs. R.'s bed, so that when lying down her face was almost directly opposite this door and not more than ten or twelve feet from it. The lamp, which burned brightly all night, stood on a small table in the corner of the room directly opposite the door; and Ida occupied a couch against the wall and between the lamp and door.

"Mrs. Wilson was pretty well worn out with her long vigil; believing that Mrs. Rogers was dying, she was naturally very nervous and timid; and having heard Mrs. R. speak frequently of seeing her departed friends, etc., she had a feeling of expectancy and dread with regard to supernatural visitations. Between 2:00 AM and 3:00 AM, while her daughter was asleep, and while she was resting on the settee, but wide awake, she happened to look toward the door into the adjoining chamber and saw a man

standing exactly in the doorway, the door being kept open all the time. He was middle-sized, broad-shouldered, with shoulders thrown back, had a florid complexion, reddish brown hair, beard, and was bareheaded, and wore a brown sack overcoat, which was unbuttoned. His expression was grave, neither stern nor pleasant, and he seemed to look straight at Mrs. Wilson, and then at Mrs. Rogers without moving. Mrs. Wilson supposed, of course, that it was a real man, tried to think how he could have got into the house. Then, as he remained quite motionless, she began to realize that it was something uncanny, and becoming frightened, turned her head away and called her daughter, who was still asleep on the couch, awakening her. On looking back at the door after an interval of a minute or two the apparition had disappeared; both its coming and going were noiseless, and Mrs. Rogers remained perfectly quiet, and so far as could be known entirely unconscious during this time. The chamber into which this door leads being quite dark, there was no opportunity to observe whether or not the apparition was transparent. Mrs. Wilson shortly afterward went into this chamber and the living room, but did not examine the lower part of the house until morning, when the doors were found properly locked and everything all right."

Since both Mrs. Wilson and her daughter saw the apparition, I consider this to be a shared death experience. Nurse Wilson—and later Professor Crosby—went to great pains to identify the apparition. Wilson looked at photos of Mrs. Rogers' late husband as well as photos of neighbors who had died. None of them fit the description of the man seen by her and her daughter.

Angels at the bed

In the following case presented by Barrett, a number of events take place that fit into the elements of the shared death experience that I outlined in the previous chapter. For one, the spirit of a child who is dying visits a beloved cousin who does not know she is dying. In addition to this premonition of the cousin's death, the mother hears music at the moment of her child's death. Here is the story as told to Barrett by an investigator:

"Mrs. G., with her two little girls, Minnie and Ada, of the respective ages of eight and nine years, had been staying in the country on a visit to her sister-in-law, but having taken a house near London, she sent the two children with their nurse off by an early train, following herself by one a few hours later. Toward the evening of the same day, one of the little girls walked into the room of the house which they had quitted in the morning, where a cousin to whom she was much attached was sitting at his studies, and said to him, 'I am come to say good-bye, Walter; I shall never see you again.' Then kissing him she vanished from the room. The young man was greatly startled and astonished, as he had himself seen both the little girls and their nurse off by the morning train.

"At this very time of the evening both the children in London were taken suddenly sick, while playing in their new home, a few hours after they had arrived. The doctor called in

and pronounced their complaint to be smallpox of the most ma-
lignant kind. They both died within the week, but the youngest,
Minnie, died first. The day after she was buried, the poor be-
reaved mother was anxiously watching the last hours of the one
still left, for whom she well knew no chance of life remained.
Suddenly the sick child woke up from a kind of stupor, and ex-
claimed, 'Oh, look, Mamma, look at the beautiful angels!' point-
ing to the foot of the bed. Mrs. G. saw nothing, but heard soft
sweet music, which seemed to float in the air. Again the child
exclaimed: 'Oh, dear Mamma, there is Minnie! She has come for
me'; she smiled and appeared greatly pleased.

At this moment Mrs. G. distinctly heard a voice say, 'Come,
dear Ada, I am waiting for you!' The sick child smiled once again
and died without a struggle."

Undesigned coincidence

In his book, Barrett writes a commentary about why
deathbed visions—including ones I consider to be shared
death experiences—are likely true and not made up. "In
considering the value of evidence for supernormal phenomena the importance of the cumulative character of the
evidence must be taken into account," Barrett points out.
"It is the undesigned coincidence of witnesses who have
had no communication with each other that constitutes its
value taken as a whole, whilst a single case may be doubt-
ful or disproved."

He quotes Richard Whately, the former Anglican
Archbishop of Dublin, who said: "It is evident that when

many coincide in their testimony (where no previous concert can have taken place), the probability resulting from this concurrence does not rest on the supposed veracity of each considered separately, but on the improbability of such an agreement taking place by chance For [sic] though in such a case each of the witnesses should be considered as unworthy of credit, and even much more likely to speak falsehood than truth, still the chances would be infinite against their all agreeing in the same falsehood."

All of this is to say that it would be virtually impossible for these experiences to be fabricated. How could they be? The dying and the living had no opportunity to "make up" the visionary encounter they were going to experience.

Deathbed visions are different from shared death experiences. Rather than being experienced by only one person, shared death experiences are experienced by at least two people; one of them stands on the brink of death and is quite ill, and the other is quite healthy and merely waiting at the deathbed for their friend or relative to leave this mortal coil.

Supernatural dimension

This one simple fact—one person being near death and the other person(s) being healthy—sets shared death experiences apart from all other deathbed episodes. Why? Because the shared death experience corroborates that an incident of supernatural dimension has taken place.

For example, here is a case study from the proceedings of the Society for Psychical Research from the early 1900s. This is the testimony of two people sitting at the deathbed of their sister, both of whom saw the faces of their late brothers, who had obviously come to fetch their sister into the afterlife:

"In one case, two women watching by their dying sister, Charlotte, saw a bright light and within it two young faces hovering over the bed, gazing intently at Charlotte; the elder sister recognized these faces as being two of her brothers, William and John, who had died when she was young. The two sisters continued to watch the faces till they gradually 'faded away like a washed-out picture,' and shortly afterward their sister Charlotte died."

Barrett's work contained many predictive shared death experiences, ones in which people at the deathbed and others many miles away, all respond to the same experiences. For example, Barrett collected an account of a deaf-mute named John Britton, who had become ill with rheumatic fever. His hands had become so swollen with the disease that he had difficultly speaking through sign language to his family members.

The doctor, thinking Britton was going to die, suggested that the family prepare itself. A day later, several family members were sitting in the living room when they heard the sound of music coming from Britton's room. The four members of the family immediately went upstairs to see where the music was coming from. Mr. S. Allen, the steward of Haileybury College and a member of the Britton family, told investigators what happened:

"We found Jack lying on his back with his eyes fixed on the ceiling, and his face lighted up with the brightest of smiles. After a little while Jack awoke and used the words 'heaven' and 'beautiful' as well as he could by means of his lips and facial expression. As he became more conscious he also told us in the same manner that his brother Tom and his sister Harriet were coming to see him. This we considered very unlikely as they lived some distance off, but shortly afterward a cab drove up from which they alighted. They had sent no intimation of their coming, nor had anyone else. After Jack's partial recovery, when he was able to write or converse upon his fingers, he told us that he had been allowed to see into heaven and to hear the most beautiful music."

Allen asks, "How did John know that Tom and Harriet were traveling, and how could he have heard these musical sounds which we also heard?" He remarks that the music could not have come from next door or from the street. And he gives a rough plan of his house to show that it was not in a row, and that the sounds could not have been due to any normal cause.

Mrs. Allen confirmed her husband's statement. She said that she heard the sounds of singing, which came from her brother's bedroom, and that when she entered the bedroom he was in a comatose state and smiling, and his lips were moving as if he were in conversation with someone, but no sound came from them. Mrs. Allen continued, "When he had recovered sufficiently to use his hands he told me more details of what he had seen, and used the words 'beautiful music.'"

When her brother died a few years later, Mrs. Allen said, "The nurse and I were watching in the room, my brother was looking just as he did on the former occasion, smiling, and he said quite distinctly and articulately 'Angels' and 'Home.'"

Walt Whitman came to visit

Among the most fascinating shared death experiences in Barrett's work is one related to the death of American poet Horace Traubel. Lieutenant Colonel L. Moore Cosgrave, who had been with Traubel during the final three days of his life, relayed the story. The military man said that he became intrigued at the intensity by which the poet was staring at a point in the room. Cosgrave began to focus on the same point, when, he declared:

"Slowly the point at which we were both looking grew gradually brighter, a light haze appeared, spread until it assumed bodily form, and took the likeness of Walt Whitman, standing upright beside the bed, a rough tweed jacket on, an old felt hat upon his head and his right hand in his pocket . . . [H]e was gazing down at Traubel, a kindly, reassuring smile upon his face, he nodded twice as though reassuringly, the features quite distinct for at least a full minute, then gradually faded from sight."

Traubel said that he indeed saw Whitman, and even felt the great American poet touch his hand, feeling, as he described it, "as though I had touched a low electric charge."

Unfortunately, Barrett was unable to provide any theories or assessments of the case studies he provided in his book. Before *Death Bed Visions* was completed, Barrett died, or "passed into that little-known country," as the book's editor wrote in the introduction. Still, Barrett's work did show certain features in deathbed experiences that are in keeping with my findings, namely that deathbed visions have common characteristics such as radiant lights, scenes of heavenly beauty, beings of light, and feelings of great peace. And, that many at the bedside are able to share these parting visions with the person who is dying. It is also clear from reading the case studies that belief in religion or an afterlife is not required. The experience is the same whether one believes in God or not.

A modern William Barrett

Perhaps the modern version of Sir William Barrett is Peter Fenwick, MD, a fellow of the Royal College of Psychiatrists in Great Britain who is a leading authority on deathbed experiences. Fenwick has collected and analyzed hundreds of deathbed experiences. And among those he has found some shared death experiences—four to be exact, three of which involved children or adolescents. Fenwick speculated that children might have an ability to psychically connect that older people don't have. My work doesn't reach the same conclusion, but it is possible that there are other abilities children have in this realm that overshadow those of adults.

In one of Fenwick's accounts, a child of five was taken to see her grandmother as she lay dying. The child was mystified as to why everyone was weeping. She could see her late grandfather and dying grandmother standing by the bed looking happy as they waited for their departure. In another account, a mother wrote that her thirteen-year-old saw the white figure of a woman at the foot of her husband's bed. Both thought it was someone who had come to guide him to the other side.

Some of Fenwick's adult accounts are quite extensive. Here is one from a Valerie Bowes, who was at the bedside of her dying mother when she had a remarkable vision:

"It was the morning of 7 November 2006 when my beloved mother passed away. A care assistant was waiting at the door for us, and as we went into the room I saw a couple of female care assistants at the end of her bed and a man in a suit kneeling by the side of her bed. They all left the room and we just had time to kiss mother and tell her what a wonderful mother she had been, that we would be okay now and it was time for her to go. A couple of minutes later we noticed that her shallow breathing had completely stopped. The care assistant told us they had kept saying to my mum, 'Hold on Edith, your daughters are coming back,' and they felt that she had hung on until we got there. I happened to say to my sister, 'Who was the man kneeling by the bedside when we came in, was that the vicar?' She said, 'What man?' I said, 'The older man in the suit.' She said there was no man in the room. She asked when had he left

the room and I said I didn't really notice but assumed he had left the room when the female care assistants left, so we could say our good-byes. I did not know the man but did not feel any creepiness about him—it just seemed natural he was there. I wish I could say it was my father who had come for her, or someone else we loved who had passed on, but it was definitely no one I knew. My father died three weeks ago, and two days before he died (I had been told that there was nothing more that the doctors could do for him and he knew himself that he was dying) I was sitting in the small room in the hospital with him when I became aware of a figure standing behind me. I could see this (I think it was a man's) reflection in the glass window in front of me. I was so very aware of a presence and looked round to see whom it was, but he was gone and I never saw him again. I then began to explore what it might be and spent some time looking at the window and trying out different movements, to look for reflections and to try to ascertain a more mundane explanation for what I saw. However, it became very clear that there was indeed someone in the room with us. I am a minister of religion and thought that I might have seen Christ, but my more immediate reaction and thoughts at the time were that a relative of my dad's had come to accompany him on his last journey. I felt this strongly."

True visions, *not* hallucinations

Fenwick points out that visions seen by both the dying and the living cannot be defined as hallucinations. In fact, Fenwick doesn't truly know how to classify these experiences. As he puts it, "Using our current science, it is difficult to find any specific brain mechanism that would underpin and explain these wonderful experiences."

Much of Fenwick's work lends support to the specific elements that make up shared death experiences, which I have outlined in the previous chapter. For example, Fenwick has case studies in which a form is seen leaving the body, or light is seen to emanate from the dying individual at the point of death, or several people in the room hear heavenly music. Here is one such case that contains both music and light:

"Suddenly there was the most brilliant light shining from my husband's chest, and as this light lifted upwards there was the most beautiful music and singing voices, my own chest seemed filled with infinite joy ... Suddenly there was a hand on my shoulder and a nurse said, 'I'm sorry love. He has just gone.' I lost sight of the light and the music, I felt so bereft at being left behind."

In the course of gathering deathbed experiences for his research into their meaning, Fenwick was presented with several that included a "mist" or "smoke" that was seen forming around the dying person. We have already seen these in the case studies I collected in my research. But it is always interesting to see what examples other researchers have found, especially when they are from another culture yet share elements with those in my own work. It reaffirms my belief that, at our spiritual core, we are all the same.

Here is a case study from a nurse in England who saw both a cloud of mist that told her a patient was dead *and* witnessed the patient's family being roused from their sleep by a sudden urge to come to the hospital in the middle of the night:

"We had a male patient in a side ward: his prognosis wasn't good, although death wasn't deemed imminent. He had two relatives who had decided to stay the night, in case his condition worsened. They retired to an overnight room reserved for relatives.

"Around 3:00 AM, myself and the other nurse on duty were chatting at the nurse's station. The station was illuminated by a single light. I saw a white mist at the end of the nurse station. It was there and it was gone. I immediately thought of a fire, perhaps from the kitchen a little way down the corridor. I walked to one end of the ward and my colleague went to the other end. She checked the side rooms and hurried to find me to say the man in question had died, seemingly only just.

"We hurriedly phoned the Night Sister to urgently rouse the sleeping relatives. While waiting for them to appear, more relatives of the deceased arrived. They told us they had woken suddenly at home and just felt the urge to visit the hospital, feeling something was wrong."

Here is another case involving both light and smoke, this one from a personal letter to Fenwick:

"When I awoke, the room was pitch dark, but above Dad's bed was a flame licking the top of the wall against the ceiling...as I looked...I saw a plume of smoke rising, like the vapour that rises from a snuffed-out candle, but on a bigger

scale . . . it was being the thrown off by a single blade of phos-
phorous light . . . it hung above Dad's bed, about eighteen inches
or so long, and was indescribably beautiful . . . it seemed to ex-
press perfect love and peace. Eventually I switched on the light.
The light vanished and the room was the same as always on a
November morning, cold and cheerless, with no sound of breath-
ing from Dad's bed. His body was still warm."

Fenwick believes that these "mist-ical" experiences may in fact be what the dying themselves see. As he points out, many cultures see dying as dissolution, a state in which a person breaks up into smaller constituents. He refers to Tibetan beliefs, in which there are several stages of dying, including one the Dalai Lama describes as being "like blue puffs of smoke. It is similar to smoke billowing from a chimney in the midst of a mass of smoke."

Poetic and real

This may sound like a metaphoric representation of what goes on in death, but I am inclined to believe it is real and not just poetic. All of these beliefs exist for a reason, which is that the elements that compose them have been observed enough times to become gospel. They are too bizarre to have been created out of whole cloth. I believe that Tibetans witnessed the mist or smoke coming from a dying person enough times to make it a significant part of their beliefs about death and dying.

In one of his lectures on the subject of paranormal phenomena, Fenwick makes some interesting points about the role of deathbed visions—the type I would call shared death experiences—in our modern world. "A reductionist explanation of deathbed visions would be that they are simply hallucinations interpretable in terms of a change in brain chemistry, or psychologically derived, confirming expectations or providing comfort as the dying approach their death," he says. "A point against this is that occasionally visions of a dead relative appear who the dying person does not know is dead. However, caregivers witness some phenomena surrounding the deathbed, and the mechanism for these is clearly different. A reductionist view would be that they are in response to the stress that the carer has had in the months leading up to the death and are probably mediated by a change in affect. Expectations could also play a part, as death always occurs within a culture and in Western culture the concept of soul and a departure to heaven of peace and love is common. However, as we now move toward post-modern science, together with the recognition that as yet neuroscience has no explanation of consciousness (subjective experience), the possibility of transcendent phenomena around the time of death should also be considered."

The work presented above, combined with my own, leads to my belief that shared death experiences are events that take us closer to proof of an afterlife than any other event, even the near-death experience.

I know this belief leaves me open to controversy and criticism, both of which I accept willingly. As the

German philosopher Goethe said, "In the sciences...if anyone advances anything new...people resist with all their might; they speak of the new view with contempt, as if it were not worth the trouble of even so much as an investigation or a regard; and thus a new truth may wait a long time before it can win its way."

"Men love to wonder, and that is the seed of science."
—RALPH WALDO EMERSON

6

QUESTIONS ABOUT SHARED DEATH EXPERIENCES

AT THIS POINT IN THE BOOK, you undoubtedly have many questions that have not yet been answered. During my lectures I always include a question-and-answer period at the end of my talk and am inundated with a variety of questions. In this chapter I answer the ten questions that come up most often in my lectures. Keep in mind that as myself and others do more research, these answers will change and the questions will become more plentiful. The old adage holds true: For every question that is answered, many more will arise.

✧ ✧ ✧

Do shared death experiences tell us more about the afterlife than near-death experiences?

Shared death experiences tell us far more about the afterlife than do near-death experiences. I will even go so far as to say that the notion of an afterlife came from experiences like these. In other words, ancient man most likely witnessed the world of the afterlife when he experienced it during a near-death experience, and then told the tribe what he saw on the other side. Many of them undoubtedly went to the other side through shared death experiences and recounted this other dimension of reality through a loved one's death. For example, some Egyptologists believe that Egyptian religion had its roots in the telling of near-death experiences among various tribes. Gradually, when the tribes realized that the stories were all the same, they unified behind common religious beliefs that are etched and painted on the walls of ancient Egyptian ruins. Certainly most of what was recounted were near-death experiences brought about by near drownings in the Nile or animal attacks, but it is logical to assume that some of these stories were also shared death experiences.

I think these shared death experiences open up an entirely new avenue of rational enlightenment on the question of life after death. They also open a new avenue for scientific studies. And as these studies are completed, it will become clear that shared death experiences are the key to proving the existence of an afterlife.

Why do I think that? Because shared death experiences eliminate what I call the escape clause of belief. Here is what I mean: Until now, near-death experiences have been considered the best proof of life after death. But many people believe—and this is the escape clause—that a near-death experience is nothing but hallucination caused by a lack of oxygen to the brain, or fear, or too much anesthetic, or not enough anesthetic. You get the picture. Some people will go to any length to deny that near-death experiences can provide a view of what we call "the afterlife." So they say the near-death experience is just a hallucination at the point of death—a physiological phenomenon.

But doubters can't say that with a shared death experience. Why? Because the people who report these experiences are not near death. They are generally sitting at the deathbed of a loved one when they suddenly have one of these marvelous and puzzling experiences. And it's the very fact that they aren't near death that negates the escape clause. Shared death experiences happen to healthy people, which is why it is so important to explore them. Since their experiences are not just the result of bad brain chemistry, we will have to go beyond that argument. Shared death experiences are going to force people to come up with a whole new framework for rational discussion of the afterlife.

Are men or women more likely to have shared death experiences?

This is not intended to be a sexist question. Rather, this is a question that has been asked since near-death studies began. It's a fair question, and one that has been asked of me many times by women and men alike. The assumption is that women are more empathic and sensitive to their environment than men, and therefore are more likely to have near-death experiences as well as to sense other types of supernatural events, including the near-death experiences of others.

My experiences and observation over a long period of time convince me that males and females have such experiences about equally, but that women, at least as far as I can now tell, are a little more open to talking about them. It is usually not until I sit down face-to-face with a man who has had a shared death experience that he begins to talk about it. I have found men to be more awkward in talking about spiritual matters, but when they do, they usually speak very fluidly about their experiences. Why? Some men experience emotions as a form of weakness. As a result they really don't like to reveal them to a stranger. I have also found that men think they have more to lose by talking about these experiences, that somehow a discussion about such a subject will result in them being ostracized by their peer group. What many men don't realize is that many in their peer group have had the same or similar experiences.

A great example of this came to me from a doctor in the Midwest. He worked in a busy emergency room and sometimes performed several cardiopulmonary resuscitations per week. Sometime in his early forties, this doctor began to see a mist or cloud rise from a person who was dying. The first two times he saw this were with patients who died before he could begin CPR. Then he began to see this mist during resuscitation, and more than once he saw a transparent figure leave a body that he was working on.

Needless to say, the doctor was frightened by these events. But he was also curious. Did his colleagues see this mist too? Did they see what seemed to be the person's spirit leave as the physical body died?

Cautiously, this doctor began to ask discreetly among his colleagues. Most of them had never heard of such a phenomenon, while others shrugged and said it may have happened to them. When he pressed them, they referred him to an older doctor who was highly regarded by everyone on the staff.

An appointment was made and before long the young doctor found himself sitting across a desk from the older doctor, telling him about the supernatural events that had taken place. Partway through the younger doctor's account, the older doctor began to smile. Then he interrupted his young colleague in mid-sentence.

"I guess I would say, 'Welcome to the club,'" said the older doctor, offering his hand to the younger. For the next hour or so, the two of them traded stories about similar events they'd had with dying patients.

"I wish I had spoken up sooner," said the younger doctor. "It was clear that other doctors had at least heard of these events, since they were able to refer me to someone who had actually had some himself. And it was a relief to find someone who openly discussed these life-changing experiences."

The good news is that it is no longer as difficult to talk to a man about these intimate spiritual experiences as it used to be. Back in the sixties, when I first began researching near-death experiences, it was rare to find a man who would share such an experience with me at all. Society hadn't awakened to the reality of near-death experiences, and most men weren't about to share this strange experience with anyone, let alone a stranger.

I can't blame them. Shared death experiences and near-death experiences are so extraordinary that they go well outside the boundaries of everyday life. And because of that, many men just feel reluctant to talk about them.

There is another factor, too, that is very prevalent in human nature, and that is we tend to think our "odd experiences" apply uniquely to ourselves. I have found this to be particularly true of men. So when they have something like a shared death experience, they tend to assume that they may be the only one that has ever had it, and they keep it to themselves. So I think that, by and large, just because they're aware that many people won't receive it with open arms, that they are circumspect about who they tell about it. That will all change with this book. Now that people know they aren't alone, they will not be reluctant to talk about such experiences.

How do you know people aren't lying about their shared death experience?

Well, sometimes people *do* lie to you. As a person who has a background in forensic psychiatry and a human being who has lived sixty-five years, I can often tell when someone is not telling the truth. How? One way I can tell that a person is untruthful is that they will generally answer quickly and in a way that is clearly aimed at pleasing the interviewer (me).

There are other factors too. With many of these cases, I have managed to interview the person fairly soon after the event. The idea that people would create this lie about an event they obviously held sacred (the death of a parent, for example) is not as likely. There is usually too much emotional significance in such an event.

But perhaps the main reason I believe what people tell me is that shared death experiences are a new phenomenon in the public arena. Although they have probably been around since mankind began, very, very little attention has ever been drawn to them and no one until now has truly studied them. That makes them a new phenomenon, one that is just entering the public eye. It was the same way with near-death experiences in the 1970s. Because they had not yet been talked about on a wide basis, they represented a "pure" subject, one not likely to be made up.

Does one have to be religious to have these experiences?

This is a question I have been asked many times, regarding both near-death and shared death experiences. To me, this question is meant to imply that these experiences are just fantasy brought on by years of religious training. But in fact, that is not the case. These experiences are truly cross-cultural in that they happen to people of all races, colors and creeds. Yes, even atheists.

That means that, with a near-death experience, both believers and atheists will have some version of an experience in which they leave their body, have a tunnel experience, see beings of light, have a life review, and so on. The difference, say a number of researchers, is that the religious are likely to associate the beings of light with religious figures, like God or Jesus. The atheist will likely say that they saw a being of light, period.

There are a number of studies that show the universality of near-death experiences. These studies show that one does not have to be religious to have the common elements of near-death and related experiences, in which I am including shared death experiences. The best of the studies to date is one by Jeffrey Long, MD, who, along with his wife, Jody, administers the Near Death Experience Research Foundation (NDERF). Through their organization's Web site (www.nderf.org) they have collected hundreds of near-death experiences from around the world, and have been able to draw firm conclusions from their analysis, which are published in his recent book, *Evidence of the Afterlife*. Here, in a nutshell, are their findings:

- **The core near-death experience is the same all over the world.** Whether it's had by a Hindu in India, a Muslim in Egypt, a Christian in the United States or an atheist in Iceland, the same core near-death experience elements are present in all, including: feelings of peace, out-of-body experience, tunnel experience, beings of light, a life review, reluctance to return and transformation.

- **Preexisting cultural beliefs do not influence NDEs.** Many of the people in the NDERF study did not know what a near-death experience was until years after having it. Surely, if they wanted to put a religious or cultural spin on the story, they would have done so in the interim. Few did, even in the Middle Eastern countries where religion is such an overwhelming factor. They just told the facts, with no apparent embellishment.

The research done by Long and others reveals an interesting thing about near-death experiences: They happen to everyone the same way—religious or not.

Since this book represents the first investigation of shared death experiences, we don't have the benefit of years of cross-cultural studies to indicate whether they happen in the same way to the religious and the non-religious. However, based on the case studies I have gathered and analyzed, I feel confident that the experiences of believers and non-believers are essentially the same; only the interpretation may differ.

Still, it is fair that some people might ask the following question.

Do you think people change their experiences to fit into a religious belief?

People draw words and ideas from their religious background to put shared death experiences into words and context. They have to. Since there are no words to describe what happens in a shared death experience, they're forced to put the experience into religious terminology. But at the same time, they will usually acknowledge that the terminology they use is inadequate to the situation, that what they experienced is almost ineffable. Based on that, what else can they do? When people have these kinds of powerful experiences, they try to assimilate them into existing beliefs or perspectives. That's a very natural thing to do. We have to explain them to ourselves somehow.

The idea I often hear expressed is that when people have a shared death experience, it wakes them up to the fact that what they had heard in church has a basis in reality. In other words, it's not just something coming from a book or sermon. There's an immediate awareness that this is the same material that religion is made from, which is often very shocking to people.

I've spoken with many people who don't have any particular religious background, yet who are surprised that what they see in their shared death experience is the kind of imagery and events that have been talked about by their religious friends. For instance, they see beings that look like angels or see deceased relatives at the moment of their loved one's death. They describe mystical lights and moments of intense love brought on by their shared experience. This comes as a surprise to many who have no religious background or those who are atheists or otherwise hostile toward religion.

One woman who called herself a "devout non-believer" was stunned when she accompanied her husband through a bright tunnel at the moment of his death. They were headed for a light when an "angel" pulled her back and she was suddenly sitting once again at the bedside, holding her husband's hand. She was ecstatic at the experience, and it helped her accept the reality that her husband had passed. "I was raised to not believe in religion or God," she said. "But now I believe in God and in spirituality. Religion feels very manmade to me, but I can't deny the spirituality of what happened when my husband died. It has given me a peace and a belief in the afterlife that I didn't know was possible."

Non-religious people can become very confused by what they see in their brief sojourn to the other side during a shared death experience. It is not unusual to hear non-religious people say, "I saw something *like* an angel come to greet my mother," or "When I went through the tunnel with dad, it *looked like* a bunch of angels were there to meet him," or "Some people *might call* the person I saw Jesus."

It is my feeling that all experiencers—religious and non—find the same elements in their shared death experiences and struggle to put them into language. Generally speaking, they choose the language and the terminology that they are most familiar with. That said, however, I find that most Christians don't skew the facts of their experience at all. Some see Jesus or other religious figures while some don't. Period. They don't try to skew the facts to make it appear as though they were in the presence of a religious figure. For example, read these two case studies and see if you can tell that both are told by very

religious Christians. The first comes from a nurse at a
large metropolitan hospital:

*"An old man was dying in our unit, and it was a long drawn
out thing in the wee hours of the morning. I walked into his
room and there was a woman sitting beside his bed. I knew right
away she was a spirit, not a bodily person. She said nothing, just
looked at the man.*

*"I felt my heart skip beats in my chest; I was so shocked,
yet not frightened. The whole thing was so natural despite how
the words might make it seem. I was startled and just turned
around right out of the room, feeling like I had intruded on a
personal occasion.*

*"I wanted to discuss the incident with a more experienced
social worker on the ward, but before I could, she said, 'I saw her
too. Things like this happen fairly often.'*

*"I was surprised. But since then I've heard other stories like
this, where the dead are seen hovering around and waiting."*

Here is another case study, this one from a son who
was with his father as he died:

*"My dad died a peaceful death from cancer. I was there
throughout the process. Something strange happened at the end
that I still do not understand. The last four hours of his life, I
kept hearing a distinct hum or vibration, like a musical note. I
have never heard this note before or since.*

*"The note was pleasant with no variation, but it felt like mu-
sic. It was unmistakably music. The note was not coming from
my father; it was more like music was coming through him. I felt
like he and I were bundled together carrying on our conversation
in some other place, kind of between worlds.*

"It was plain that he was seeing things that I could not perceive, for example, talking to his mother who had died. The hum was something on the order of a hum in electrical equipment and literally seemed to fill the air with energy. Yet never once did I mention it to anyone else at the bedside because it was immediately apparent that this was a sound from somewhere else.

"I was holding his hand when he died, and less than a minute later, this musical note just went silent. I felt as though in that moment a kind of thread that linked me to the spirit world had been disconnected. I knew it had only been temporarily disconnected, though. That music from someplace else assured me there is a life after death, where I will see my mother and father again."

It is clear that these very religious people made no religious representation of their experience. With most who have shared death experiences, the experience itself is so powerful that embellishing it with religious imagery does not come to mind.

The truth is powerful enough.

Do people who have shared death experiences go on to communicate with the deceased?

That happens sometimes. People say that they feel that the spirit of the person "hangs around" for a period of time. But in terms of this opening a perpetual line of communication to the "other side," I have not seen that happen. For most people it's a onetime event, in the sense that this incredible experience is focused on the time of the death of the person or just a short window around it. It doesn't seem to open any sort of permanent hotline to the heaven, by any means.

One of the experiencers described it perfectly. She said, "After this experience, there is a kind of nostalgia, like a longing to experience that state of consciousness again." Many describe a kind of "homesickness." They had this experience in which the eternity came into view, and now they feel nostalgic for that state of consciousness because they are not able to get back into it by any sort of effort. One experiencer told me, "I would gladly go back to wherever I was. It was frightening and exhilarating at the same time. Definitely reduced my fear of death."

All of this is not to say that there is never post-death communication. I have heard of people who have had shared death experiences going on to communicate with the deceased. One woman told me that "virtually every alarm clock, television, radio and other electronic device" came to life the night after her grandmother died. She reported that her husband became so frightened that he smashed several of the items to keep them from coming on again. She, on the other hand, had peaceful dreams of lengthy conversations with her grandmother in which she was told not to cry.

Another vivid example of afterlife communication came from Dr. Ervin Shaw of Lexington, South Carolina, who wrote me an e-mail about the shared experience he had with his father and the communication he had with him later. Here is what Dr. Shaw wrote:

"In 1993 I was in the hospital hall when the 'code red' light came on about 4:00 AM over the closed door of my father's

hospital room. He was eighty-one and in the fifth year of his decline into death, nearly blind from macular degeneration and due for insertion of a feeding tube, an end-of-life issue over which my mother and I had strongly disagreed.

"My mother and I rushed for the door. (Daddy had had some type of sinking spell about two hours prior and was unconscious when I arrived about fifteen minutes earlier.) As the door opened, the nurse was slightly restraining him, and he was sitting up pointing straight ahead with a profoundly startled stare on his face, like . . . 'My God! Do you see what I see?' Then he sank back in the bed and was gone in another five minutes.

"I was separated from my wife and living on a houseboat and was newly and intensely back in church after a twenty-five-year hiatus. I worried whether Daddy had seen Satan.

"In the middle of the night, six to twelve months later, I guess, I was startled and instantly awakened to the sound of my father's voice, 'Bud! How are y'all down there?' The 'down there' comforted me for years, and I've never heard anything more."

Case studies like these tell me that there is possible after death communication, but nothing that consists of an "open line" of contact.

Do people in other cultures have these experiences?

Absolutely. In Italy, for example, I was speaking in a room of about two thousand people when I described shared death experiences and asked about how many in the room had had some sort of "empathic" death experience. I would estimate that nearly a hundred hands went up.

I have asked this question many times during lectures in the Western world and have found that the number of people who have heard of shared death experience or had one themselves equals about one person in twenty. Their experiences were no different from what I have heard in other countries of Europe or in America.

The same has been true in India. In my travels to that country, where I have delivered many talks, I have asked the people there about shared death experiences and have heard them recount the same types of events as people in the Western world.

Once again I refer to my experience with skeptics when I founded the field of near-death studies. The skeptics declared that there would be stark, cross-cultural differences, that people in India or Africa, for instance, would have greatly different near-death experiences from those in Italy or the United States. But that wasn't true with near-death experiences and I suspect it will prove to not be true with shared death experiences, either. The kind of stories I hear worldwide—both near-death experiences and shared death experiences—are the same kind of stories with little variation.

At this point there are no cross-cultural studies as yet related to shared death experiences. There are, however, some excellent ones that examine cross-cultural elements of near-death experiences. One of the latest and perhaps largest is an ongoing examination of thousands of near-death case studies from all over the world by Jeffrey Long of the Near Death Experience Research Foundation (NDERF).

Long found that preexisting cultural beliefs do not influence near-death experiences, that no matter the religious bent of the experiencer, no cultural spin is put on their account of what happened. He also concluded that there is no difference in near-death experiences worldwide.

Although the NDERF study relates only to near-death and not shared death experiences, I am speculating that there is no difference worldwide in shared death experiences too.

Many ancient cultures have religions or mystical ceremonies based upon revelations from near-death experiences, which, I believe, include shared death experiences too. Archaeological evidence has shown that tens of thousands of years ago, primitive man was ritualistically burying the dead and surrounding them with objects that they would need in the afterlife.

We discussed Egypt earlier, but let's address it here in depth. Long before there were pyramids or even an Egypt, the people of the Nile River Valley went to great lengths to bury their dead in the salty earth so that mummification would take place. They did this because they believed the human body consisted of two spiritual entities, the "Ba" and the "Ka." They loosely defined the "Ba" as our soul and the "Ka" our life force. Since the "Ka" needs to eat and drink after the body's death, they surrounded the corpse with food and other objects that would help sustain it for a period of time in the afterlife.

Egyptian religion contained many of the elements of near-death and shared death experiences. For example:

- The separation of the "Ka" from the "Ra" had the elements of the out-of-body experience. Scenes of the spirit leaving the body are recorded on many temple and tomb walls.
- Seeing a bright light as the deceased passed into death was reported in the Pyramid Texts and *The Egyptian Book of the Dead* and is also recorded on the walls of pharaohs' tombs.
- The "Ib," or heart, was the seat of emotions and intent. It was examined for its qualities of good and bad by the god Anubis, who passed judgment on whether its owner should be admitted into the afterlife.
- The deceased traveled through a dark tunnel to meet up with dead relatives.

Since Egypt is generally recognized as the first country to practice an organized form of resurrection religion, it is fair to ask why this culture began to believe in an afterlife. The late Cyril Aldred felt he discovered the answer. Aldred, a noted Egyptologist who served as assistant curator of the Royal Scottish Museum in Edinburgh, Scotland, studied the unification of ancient Egypt. He concluded that, in addition to being unified by new and better agricultural techniques, the various tribes were bound together spiritually by stories they told one another of friends and relatives who had nearly died from animal attacks, accidents or illness.

These stories were near-death experiences by any measure. I propose that some of these experiences were also shared death experiences, the examination of which would have led to that age-old question: What happens when we die?

Some Egyptologists think that the examination of these experiences by the ancients led to the founding of a full-blown religion, one that included the creation of gods and extensive death-related rituals, including preparation of the body for burial and poetic verses that served as a guide in the afterlife.

As the religion progressed, curiosity increased. And with that curiosity came further study. A number of Egyptologists and near-death-experience researchers have pieced information together and concluded that there was a Cult of Osiris, honoring the god of agriculture and resurrection. His enemies plotted against him and, according to the Egyptian myth that guided the ancients, captured and sealed him in a wooden chest. His eventual resurrection was seen as proof of life ever after.

The Cult of Osiris seemed to be the equivalent of a bizarre medical study, one in which slaves and volunteers were suffocated nearly to death in coffins and then questioned by priests about what they saw when they were dead. Such studies were extremely valuable in developing the ancient view of the afterlife. As noted researcher Kenneth Ring, PhD, summarized it, "[B]ecause most [resuscitated slaves] were thrust into their initiation without either purification or preparation, they may bring back a somewhat distorted version of its essential insights or, even if that is not the case, be unable truly to appreciate its significance or conduct themselves in accordance with its spiritual implications... In this light it may be useful to view the near-death experience as an initiation in the sense of a beginning rather than, as it presumably was for the Osirian initiates, the culmination of a process of spiritual development and refinement."

I agree with Dr. Ring's findings, but go a few steps further in declaring that the experiences that guided ancient Egyptians were shared death experiences too. Such knowledge of the afterlife provided powerful underpinnings for ancient Egyptian society. This knowledge can be seen on the tomb walls of Egypt, where hieroglyphs and petroglyphs depict out-of-body experiences and other key events of the near-death experience. It was through this study of death that such esoteric works as the *pert em hru*, translated as *Manifestations in the Light*, were written. Since these scrolls were most often found in tombs, the Western archaeologists who found them gave this work a name that stuck: *The Egyptian Book of the Dead*. This bible of the heavenly realm reads like a study of near-death and shared death experiences.

The end result of studying the stories of death was a religion so great that it built a society, the remnants of which live today in the form of stunning tombs, colorful hieroglyphs, and the only Wonder of the World still standing, the Great Pyramid of Giza.

There are other examples throughout history—modern and ancient—that show us how other cultures have been affected by near-death and shared death experiences. The main point I am making, though, is that cultures around the world have the same type of experiences—both shared death and near-death—and have had these experiences since very early in their history.

Do you think people are transformed by these experiences in the same way that those who actually die and then return to life are transformed by theirs?

At the beginning of my near-death research, I heard this theme of transformation constantly. I hear this to some degree with shared death experiencers, who say such things as, "This experience woke me up to life after death," or "It has made me think about things that I have never thought about," or, "I now know that I will see my loved ones again."

Typical of the transformation I see is this case study from an older woman who'd had a shared death experience more than twenty years earlier. When her husband died, she walked with him through "a misty curtain" into a field of bright light. She described what happened next as being both remarkable and transformative:

"We had a flashback of our life together. The event that stood out the most was our wedding day. We stood in front of the priest

who said we would be together until 'death do us part,' which
had just taken place. I had a deep sense of what that meant and
felt the strong loyalty and love that it took to be able to stay in
love for so long.

"There was very beautiful music at this point, a heavenly
choir. The room was so bright that the only people I could really
see well were my husband and his father.

"Until this point in my life I have had doubts about life after
death. But after this happened I have had no doubts at all. I miss
my husband a lot, even after all of these years, but I know I'll
be with him again someday and knowing that puts my mind at
ease. People say I have changed for the better after this experi-
ence and I would agree. How could it be any other way? I saw
heaven and came back. Such a thing touches a person."

Powerful events like these are transformative. Even
years after a person has had a shared death experience,
they will tell me how the event changed their life. Typical
of these comments are:

- "I now realize that there is life after death, and I have
  no doubt in my mind that I will see my husband
  again."
- "I no longer fear life or am I afraid that I will run out
  of time. When I crossed over with my father I could
  see that life continues on and our consciousness super-
  sedes our physical body."
- "I quit taking life so seriously when I saw what I did as
  my wife died. We are here to learn and then we go on.
  We are not in some kind of dead-end experience here."

One of the finest examples of transformation through a shared death experience came to me from a woman who was with her sisters at their grandmother's deathbed. She tells the story beautifully, from the bright light that permeated the room, to the uncontrollable laughter that possessed the sisters, to the transformation that has taken place as a result of this experience. Here is what she says:

"My sisters and I were standing at the bedside of our grandmother, Nana, who had been in a coma for the last several days. Although ninety-seven, she had just recently fallen ill with heart failure, and almost immediately went into a coma.

"She was still in her own bed, in her own home, as we had always promised her. The hospice nurse was due to stop by at anytime to check on her. We were just gathered around her bed talking to her and to each other, having no idea that her death was happening then. For no apparent reason we all started to laugh and became really giddy. We started saying silly and funny things to her and to each other. We could not stop laughing; the room seemed to get lighter and lighter, but a different light than from a light bulb...from some other source. It was bright but it did not hurt your eyes at all. The room also began to vibrate a bit, or maybe to shake a little; at the same time it seemed to change shape. It was still her bedroom, the one I had known all my life, but it seemed to take on a spiral shape, it got longer and rounder. We all felt it. In a funny way it was a bit like being tipsy, but, of course, we weren't.

"When the hospice nurse came in, she smiled at us like she saw this kind of thing every day, a bunch of girls standing around their dying grandmother's bed laughing their heads off.

The nurse began to take our grandmother's vital signs; she said, 'You better go and get the rest of your family now. Her time has come.' We all had tears rolling down our cheeks, but tears of joy, not sadness. It was like she was laughing with us. I could hear her—not in my head so much, as in my heart.

"When my dad, Nana's son, walked in the room, I could tell that he thought we had lost our minds. You could see it from the look on his face. Whatever we felt, he could not or did not feel it. But the warmth and laughter we shared at the moment of her death just felt so right. It is something that has always stayed with my sisters and me and I realized that day, there truly is a heaven, and that Nana was on her way there, while leaving us a tiny slice—or maybe a peek—of it here.

"It changed my life, and the lives of each of us who were with her at the end to witness the pure joy of what they call 'going home.' Now I understand what that means, and I think of that day as the greatest gift that Nana could ever give us, one of happiness and joy—hers and ours, not sadness at her passing. Although we still miss her so much, we know that we will all be there together someday, without a doubt. Now, I know we will be reunited."

Comments like these are all indications that a profound transformation has taken place in the psyche of those who have shared death experiences.

Why do some people have a shared death experience and others don't?

I really don't have any idea. But it's a similar situation with near-death experiences. Why do some individuals have near-death experiences and others don't? Even when the circumstances of their "close calls" with death and their personalities are very similar, I just don't know why that would be.

I wish I could answer that question, because that is the fundamental one! I mean, if you answer that one question, it would answer a whole host of questions about telepathy, life after death, apparitions, out-of-body experiences, and virtually every other query in the field of paranormal studies. Do some people have something, an area of the brain perhaps, that allows them to have closer contact with supernatural states? The answer to that question would be a great leap forward for science.

But with shared death experiences you have to remember that the mind of the percipient may have nothing to do with having the experience. Rather, it might be the mind of the person who is dying or the dying state itself that communicates events to the mind of a bystander in a telepathic manner.

As you can see, shared death experiences open up some new fields of inquiry, ones that will be examined in-depth in years to come. They are the next step in what is loosely known as near-death studies, the continuum of paranormal and spiritual exploration.

People like to categorize things, to put them in boxes. This is fine, but we must remember that all extra-normal experiences involving the dying process are connected. That doesn't mean they aren't different—they are. But they have enough common elements in them to link them into a continuum—a series of things that blend into one another so seamlessly that it is difficult to see where one becomes the other.

Such is the case with near-death experiences and shared death experiences. Each has many of the same elements, like out-of-body experiences, tunnel experiences, visions of heaven, and beings of light. It can no longer be said that these elements belong only to the near-death experience. Instead they are all part of a spectrum that emanates from extra-normal experiences. An example of what I mean comes from an anesthesiologist in Florida. As you will see, he had a shared death experience. But in addition to that, he had communication with what he calls an angel before the shared death experience. These two experiences belong in entirely different disciplines unless they are considered to be in the same continuum.

Here, in the anesthesiologist's own words, is his story:

"I am not a touchy-feely person. I care deeply for people but I keep my emotions in check, which is a necessary quality in anesthesiology.

"I am very active in civic causes and I focus on shelters for abused women and children because my father was a severe alcoholic. I also love God with all my heart, but I believe that organized religion is a social activity more than something that gives me a spiritual benefit. My real communication with God is personal, and I speak to him on a consistent basis throughout the day.

"I tell you this just so you'll know something about my background and beliefs leading up to the experience I am going to tell you.

"As you know, anesthesiologists routinely go to the patient a day before surgery to introduce themselves and familiarize the patient with the next day's procedure. One day while I was making the rounds of the hospital, I distinctly heard an angel talk to me. I had just finished talking to a patient and was standing in the hall making notations on his chart when I heard a voice say, 'Go into the next room to your left and see the man in there. He needs you.' This doesn't happen very much so I wrote down what I heard word-for-word and then I walked right into the next room.

"As soon as I came in I could hear the patient's labored breathing. I knew he had a DNR order (Do Not Resuscitate), and I could tell that his time was near. I walked over to him and could see a look of abject horror in his eyes. Before I could say anything, he said in a raspy voice, 'I'm dying. I'm so scared I don't know what to do. Please help me.'

"When he said that I heard the angel again saying, 'Don't worry. You'll go across with him.'

"When I reached down and touched the man's hand, we crossed into another dimension and into a passageway of some kind. I have no idea if I was out of body or not; we just kept flowing toward something I cannot describe. The man looked happy and he was surrounded by other presences. I think they were family members but I couldn't ask. He didn't look at me in this place. He knew it wasn't any of my business.

"I turned my attention away from the whole thing and right away found myself back at the bedside right next to the man's dead body. I knelt next to the bed and thanked God for the experience."

As you can see, the man had contact with an angel and then he went on to have a shared death experience. Although they are two completely different types of experiences, we don't really have any rational basis for "drawing the line" between experiences. All forms of supernatural experiences—shared death experiences, near-death experiences, and many others—consist of so many of the same elements that they should be researched together and considered almost one and the same.

Is it possible to prime oneself for a shared death experience? In other words, are there things I can do to make a shared death experience happen?

Without further research it is difficult to say for sure whether you can make yourself more likely to have a shared death experience. However, some of the case studies I have collected have common elements that seem to make the shared death experience more likely. A well-developed sense of empathy is one such element that most of the experiencers seem to have. Another such element is a sense of acceptance or surrender that the loved one is going to die. This, too, is a common element in many of the case studies and makes me think that acceptance might well be one of the doors to having such an experience.

A beautiful example of acceptance leading to a shared death experience comes to me from Dr. Joan Borysenko, a Harvard University psychologist and author of several books, including the classic *Minding the Body, Mending the Mind*.

Borysenko's mother was dying at the age of eighty-one, and Joan was pushing her mother back to her room after she had refused to have a diagnostic X-ray. The refusal had been somewhat comic. When the mother found that the X-ray was to assess the level of internal bleeding that was going on, she raised herself up on one arm and challenged the doctor. "You mean I've been laying here all of these hours just because you needed a diagnosis?" she asked in a tone that wilted the physician. "Why didn't you just ask me? I'm dying! How's that for a diagnosis?"

With a weak wave of her hand, she insisted that her daughter push her gurney back to her room so she could die in peace. As Joan pushed her mother into the elevator for the eight-floor ride to her room, she reflected on the rocky relationship that the two had always had. Despite Joan's obvious accomplishments, being a Harvard University professor of psychology wasn't enough for her mother. She wanted her daughter to marry a wealthy Jewish man and live a life with fewer challenges than the academic one she had chosen. This "difference in life scripts," as Joan described it, had always led to a great deal of tension between mother and daughter. But now as they rode silently up the slow elevator at what is now Beth Israel Deaconess Medical Center, Joan realized that the woman she could call her greatest challenge was about to die. Apparently her mother realized the same thing, because she spoke first. "You know, Joan, in many ways I have not been a good mother," she said. "And I want you to know that I love you and I hope that you can for-give me."

Joan's heart opened. For the remainder of the elevator ride she confessed that she, too, had not been such a great daughter. Yet despite the times that she had been judg-mental, ungrateful and unkind, she told her mother that she had always loved her. Then, before the elevator door opened and they took their last walk together, Joan asked her mother if they could exchange a soul quality.

Her mother had always mocked talk like this in the past, but on her last day she was already shifting and she asked for her daughter's greatest quality: compas-sion. Joan gave her that compassion and asked for courage in return. "You're one tough cookie, Mom. You don't crumble."

In the course of an elevator ride, the two had become, well, *elevated*. Along with her son and brother, Joan spent the next several hours having a very sweet time with her dying mother. At one point she asked everyone to leave because "it's hard to die with all of this love here." They refused. Instead they chose to sing songs and recall mo-ments of her life while she smiled.

After midnight, her mother slipped into a morphine-induced sleep and began to drift off toward death. As that happened, Joan felt her consciousness shift until she re-alized she was out of her body. Then she entered a light, had a life review—first of her own life, in which she saw all of her good and bad deeds, and then of her life with her mother.

"I saw unpleasant things—fights we had with each other and mind games that we played," said Joan. "But this life review was coming out of this light and the light told us that it was clear that we were both teachers to one another."

At a certain point, the scenes ended, followed by feelings of complete gratefulness and connection. It was, as Joan said, "a feeling like my mother had given me birth into this physical realm while I had given birth to her soul out of this physical realm."

Joan felt—as do I after hearing her story—that it was the moment of surrender in the elevator that was the key to this shared death experience. Without that moment of surrender I doubt that this experience would have taken place. But with it, the mother and daughter were able to get rid of the baggage that had weighed down their relationship and they were able to connect in a way that they had not before.

Does that mean such factors as surrender are necessary for a shared death experience to take place? Most in my field would say that "more research is necessary," but I am willing to say that empathy and surrender are definitely among the keys that can lead to this marvelous experience.

Exactly what is meant by "surrender"? For some people, surrender could be defined in religious terms. In James 4:7, the apostle instructs, "Submit yourself, then, to God," which to me means that you accept God's will, which in this case might well be the death of a loved one. Whether one chooses a religious interpretation or not, the definition of surrender is largely the same: accept what is happening and give yourself to the person who is dying. Accepting what is can open a person to many possibilities of what can be.

Surrender requires tremendous strength. It is not giving up. Joseph Campbell summed it up nicely when he said: "We must be willing to let go of the life we have planned, so as to have the life that is waiting for us." Achieving surrender opens you to a divine energy, one that many know as grace. By opening to the power of grace, one opens themselves to a number of new and powerful spiritual experiences.

> *"The seat of faith ... is not consciousness but spontaneous religious experience, which brings the individual's faith into immediate relation with God."*
> —CARL JUNG

7

✧✧✧

EXPLANATIONS

As MUCH AS I UNDERSTAND the reality of shared death experiences, I also realize that we are a long way from explaining what they are and how it is that they take place. This does not bother me. I think it is good for mankind to have a hearty dose of the unexplained. To my way of thinking, shared death experiences and other such supernatural events are similar to the northern lights, that ethereal glow that takes place near the North Pole. It wasn't until 2008 that the conditions that trigger these hallucinogenic acts of nature were finally determined. That doesn't mean people didn't admire their wonder before 2008. The Northern Lights have been a source of awe for mankind despite—or perhaps because of—their unexplained nature. The same is true of near-death experiences, which, although they have never been fully explained, are a source of awe and wonder for most everyone who has knowledge of them.

We are a long way from explaining shared death experiences, a lack of explanation that I find a good thing. What the world needs now is an unexplainable mystery, one that offers great hope. With shared death experiences we have such an astonishing phenomenon that is verifiable by almost anyone who honestly examines it, yet is even more difficult to explain than its more familiar cousin, the near-death experience.

Still, I understand that some people have a desire—a need actually—to try and explain as much of the natural and supernatural world as they can. And I do accept that there are those who believe that the supernatural is merely the natural that is not yet explained.

Given this desire to explain the supernatural world, I will address what I think will become the common explanations for shared death experiences, offering my interpretation of each. As I have already said, no explanation is truly possible at this point, and I am fine with that. Experiences like these unfold over time and reveal what they reveal. There are researchers out there who will attempt to hurry these revelations with scientific studies. I wish them well. I am more patient than that. For me, I will bathe in the astonishment of these experiences for some time before coming to any solid conclusions of my own. They will tell me about themselves in due time. In the meantime, I will present some of what will likely be the dominant explanations for these amazing shared experiences.

✧✧✧

Empathic System

In a moment of candor, David Attenborough, the famed British naturalist known to many for playing the man who created a dinosaur habitat in the movie *Jurassic Park*, told a journalist why he could not deny the existence of God. "Often when I open a termite's nest and see thousands of blind organisms working away, that lack the sense mechanism to see me, I can't help thinking maybe there's a sense mechanism I'm missing, that there's someone around who created this and I just can't perceive him," he said. "We cannot discount that."

The notion of a missing sense mechanism is very relevant to the study of shared death experiences. As we know, the human race is blessed with five basic senses: sight, touch, taste, smell and hearing. It was Aristotle who categorized these in the third century BC, so it's no wonder that modern science has since added even more, including a sense of balance, pain, temperature difference and even direction. Scientists have added even more, including such senses as chemoreception (the body's ability to detect chemical change and react to it) and photoreception (nerve cells in the eye that turn light into sight).

Shared death experiences deal with the notion of a variety of extra senses, including telepathy, clairvoyance, remote viewing, astral projection, spontaneous out-of-body

experiences and perhaps others that I have not yet antici-
pated. As the psychologist Carl Jung said, "The meeting
of two personalities is like the contact of two chemical
substances: if there is any reaction, both are transformed." By the very nature of that transformation between two people at a time of extreme stress and
difficult conditions, undiscovered senses may be coming
into play.

I can't begin to say what these senses might be, but
I can speculate on a number of possibilities, hoping that
such speculation will begin a dialogue about the possibility of an undiscovered realm of the senses that presents
itself at the point of death, or before.

One sense that might be related to such phenomena as
shared death experiences is our brain's empathic system.
This system is composed of mirror neurons; brain cells
that fire when we watch someone else perform even subtle acts. This neuron, according to researcher Barbara Wild
at the University of Tübingen in Germany, allows people
to "feel a pale reflection of their companions' actual emotions," allowing them into the emotional lives of others. It
is mirror neurons that explain why happiness can be contagious or why depression can sweep through a college
dormitory. Or even why a crabby bank teller can make a
customer feel suddenly cranky too.

Mirror neurons explain why happiness, obesity, smoking and drinking, even suicidal behavior, are sometimes a
social force and not always decided by an individual. They
tell us why we become the company we keep by picking
up the traits of those we work or play with, even traits we
wouldn't normally have.

It might also be mirror neurons that explain shared death experiences. It is through these neurons that a form of thought transfer might take place at the moment of death, allowing the dying person's thought and feelings to become available to a person who is truly empathic.

A retired philosophy professor in his seventies gave me just such an example. When he was a boy of eight, he was sitting on the kitchen floor of his family's farmhouse in the Midwest. As he played happily with a toy truck, his grandmother stood at the kitchen stove, cooking dinner. Said the professor:

"Grandma made a noise and I happened to look up at her and saw a look of discomfort and incomprehension on her face. All of a sudden she keeled over like a fence post falling down, straight as a stick without her knees even buckling.

"I could see her dead body on the floor. But also at the same time I saw a much younger version of her standing exactly where she had been standing when she fell. Now, there was a second figure beside her who was a man about her same apparent age. The two looked at me and waved, and when they did I felt a deep love. Then they turned away as a unit and disappeared by walking away together through the kitchen wall.

"We didn't have the word 'holographic' then, but it occurs to me how that this is the best word available to characterize the experience. The two people could be described as looking like a hologram, yet they had a greater degree of reality to them than anything I have experienced before or since."

Although research into the empathic nervous system has not yet looked at the possibility of thought transfer,

I am suggesting that such a topic of study may take researchers down an interesting path. What might such researchers find? They may find that telepathy does not involve the reading of radio-like brain waves, which has been the main assumption by researchers as far back as 1882, when Fredric W.H. Myers coined the word "telepathy" to describe the concept of thought transference.

Rather, I am proposing that researchers look at something completely different from the brain wave theory. What I'm saying is that they look at the possibility that humans can communicate psychically with others through these mirror neurons, and that communication takes place via a chemical reaction in the cells and not by "picking up" some kind of projected brain wave.

The notion that telepathic communications take place as a chemical reaction is not far-fetched. Our brain cells already communicate chemically, and they do so in an instant using neurotransmitters. I am proposing that the same type of chemical communication may take place between loved ones at the point of death. Proof of the involvement of the empathic system in shared death experiences would be a tremendous step forward for both parapsychology and death studies.

In the realm of death studies it would lead to almost proof positive that one is literally sharing the death experience of another. If researchers of the empathic system can say that "actions and feelings can be as contagious as a virus" among social groups, then it's only a matter of time before they take it a step further to see if these mirror neurons can transmit other types of information.

Circuit boards of mysticism

Another possible explanation for shared death experiences comes from my friend and fellow researcher Dr. Melvin Morse. In 1988, Morse had a shared death experience when his father appeared to him from hundreds of miles away at the very moment he died. Here is Morse's recounting of that story from his book, *Parting Visions:*

> *"One night in January I came home late from the hospital. It had been a very difficult day and I was only interested in sleep. I turned off my beeper and my telephone and told my wife that I didn't want to be disturbed for any reason. Then I went to bed.*
>
> *"As I fell asleep in the darkened room, my father appeared to me in a dream. He just stood there facing me. He spoke very clearly. 'Melvin, call your answering service. I have something to tell you.'*
>
> *"I awoke with a start and charged into the living room. 'My dad just told me to call my answering service,' I said to my wife. I made the call and was told that my mother had been trying to reach me with an urgent message. It was to tell me that my father had died."*

Since that moment, Morse said he had very little doubt that the human brain has the ability to communicate telepathically. He launched into the field of near-death studies and has been one of its major researchers ever since.

He developed the concept that the right temporal lobe of the human brain is essentially "the circuit boards of mysticism." It is this area, says Morse, which allows us access to the "larger reality" of mystical consciousness.

When a mystical event takes place, says Morse, this area is most likely stimulated in some way. It is easy to see how this area could become stimulated during a near-death experience, when the brain may become hyperactive with the processes of staying conscious. But with other events (like a shared death experience) it is somewhat more difficult since it requires some kind of input from an outside source. Morse has no problem seeing it either way: "I simply think that we have a part of our brain that is in touch with what some consider to be mystical things."

Every shared death experience referenced in this book could be an example of the circuit boards of mysticism being activated. The notion that we have a "circuit board of mysticism" is a believable one to me. I think this circuit board is activated during a variety of experiences, including shared death, near-death, out-of-body and religious. This circuit board is merely our way of communicating with the divine.

Most likely Paul the Apostle was activated when he had his vision of heaven, as was that of Dr. Jonas Salk, inventor of the polio vaccine, who shocked the world when he revealed that he sat up late at night, receiving messages from another realm. *The New York Times Magazine* published an article about Salk in November 1990 in which it said that Salk fell into a "trancelike state, filling page after page in an almost indecipherable hand." He collected more than twelve thousand handwritten pages of notes that were later published in three books; *Man Unfolding, The Survival of the Wisest* and *Anatomy of Reality*. The same is true of Albert Einstein, who had a waking dream of riding a beam of light, which later became the basis for his theory of relativity.

There are those who might think that to research the connection between shared death experiences and the physiology of the human brain is an affront to God. Those who feel this way might believe that we are trying to pierce the divine veil of mystery that surrounds death, revealing the way in which God operates. I would disagree with that. In my experience, the more I have probed into the mysteries of death, the more I have found even more mystery. God lets us view his handiwork in exciting glimpses, but exactly how these experiences occur will most likely remain unseen.

As an aside, I have been the beneficiary of many such glimpses of God's handiwork. I talk to God daily and many times have had him answer, in voice and action. Shortly after my brother Randy died, both my wife and I saw him in our house. Randy appeared separately to each of us in our upstairs hallway, looking at us with a pleasant smile on his face. We both feel that this glimpse of my brother was given to us by God as a way of putting our minds at ease. Seeing my dead brother was not frightening in the least. Rather, it was comforting to see him happy and youthful after a time when we had seen him in such deep distress.

Mass hysteria

Mass hysteria takes place when more than one person demonstrates hysterical symptoms. A good example took place in the sixties, when women who worked in textile mills claimed that they became ill from being bitten by "June bugs." The U.S. Public Health Department investigated the claims and could find neither bugs nor signs of bug bites on any of the women. When their results were announced, the June bug epidemic disappeared. Another well-known example of mass hysteria took place in 1938, when thousands of people across the United States claimed they saw flashes of lightning and smelled poison gas as they listened to Orson Welles' radio adaptation of H. G. Wells' *War of the Worlds*. This was a sign of arriving spaceships in the radio play, and it took many months for these reports to die away.

I suspect that skeptics will attempt to link shared death experiences to some form of mass hysteria. But as a psychiatrist who has dealt extensively with hysterics, I can assure you that the people who have had shared death experiences that I have spoken with do not exhibit signs of hysteria, even though the conditions at the deathbed could easily lend themselves to one form or another of hysteria.

A young woman told me of an event that took place when she was fifteen years old. Her grandmother was dying in her bedroom at the family home in Montreal. The young woman—I'll call her Joyce—was in the living room watching TV, when her grandmother came into the room and said, "Come with me. Today is going to be a big day and I want to show you something." Then she led Joyce to her room, where her parents were: "My parents were surprised to see me because I had told them I was afraid to be in the room where Grandma was dying. But they were even more surprised to hear that my grandmother came and got me and led me to her room, because there was Grandma laying in the bed, at least her body was there. They said she had never left."

Joyce said she could see her grandmother get back into her body and even mentioned it to her parents as it was happening. And a few hours later as the grandmother died, Joyce told her parents that she could see her grandmother's spirit leave her body.

Picture it. There were adults who were exhausted by their long presence at the deathbed as they waited for the family matriarch to die. Suddenly their young daughter comes into the room and says Grandmother appeared to her in another room and brought her back to her body, which was lying in bed all along. Then the young girl reports that she can see the grandmother's spirit leave her body as she dies.

Such events are a perfect set-up for mass hysteria. Yet, the parents did not see the grandmother as their child did. They did not exhibit the same "symptoms" of seeing the grandmother's spirit as did their daughter.

What I am getting to is that the deathbed scene is one that lends itself to hysteria because there is a great amount of stress in being with a person as they die. On top of that, a significant amount of "wishing" goes on at the deathbed. Yet I can say with great certainty that I have rarely seen a shared death experience that even resembles mass hysteria.

Plus, there is another factor here, that being that many shared death experiences are spontaneous in that they are not connected to a lengthy wait at the deathbed. Their spontaneous nature—and that they occur independent of a deathbed scene—makes them very difficult to explain away with claims of mass hysteria.

There are several examples of the spontaneous type of shared death experience in this book, but I will provide another here as an example from a nurse in New York. This nurse worked in a hospital and among her patients was a woman named Rose, who was extremely ill with ovarian cancer. The nurse had a good relationship with Rose, but beyond reminding her of a distant aunt, there was nothing special about this patient/nurse relationship.

One morning the nurse noticed a hubbub at the distant end of the hospital hallway and she hurried down to see if she could be of any assistance. As she approached this knot of nurses, Rose emerged coming the other way. The nurse thought Rose had fled her room, disturbed perhaps by whatever was going on down there. But as Rose approached, the nurse noticed that she had a "supernatural smile" on her face.

"I was very puzzled to see happiness on her face because of all she was going through," said the nurse. "I stopped dead in my tracks and started to say something to her but she said, 'I love you. Thanks. Thank you. Can't stop now.'"

The nurse continued to the scene at the end of the hall only to find that her fellow nurses were gathered around Rose's dead body, which was slumped on the floor of her room.

Since Rose's death occurred unexpectedly and was unknown to the nurse, no stage could be set for mass hysteria or for wish fulfillment.

I discount the possibility that these shared death experiences are examples of social contagion or the emotional impact of stress, as some have declared. I have spent many hours at deathbeds and many more with people who have had these incredible experiences, and I can tell you as a psychiatrist that the deathbed scene is not one of chaos and hysteria. I can also tell you that the people who tell me their stories are not hysterics nor are they delusional. Rather, they are ordinary people who have had extraordinary experiences.

Perhaps unanswerable

When it comes to the desire to explain a phenomenon, scientists can be somewhat like children on a long road trip: Instead of looking out the window and enjoying the voyage, they are constantly concerned about getting there. The childish question, "Are we there yet?" is replaced with "Do you have an answer yet?" The answer is no, we don't have an answer yet as to what happens when we die, but we are closing in on it. The exploration of near-death experiences has taken us closer to an answer than any scientific exploration in the past. Now the study of shared death experiences will take us even further, because they are events that happen to people who are not ill or in a life-threatening situation. As a result, there can be no speculation that the experience is caused by high levels of carbon dioxide, extreme levels of drugs or even fear. The fact that the person who has a shared death experience was lucid throughout the experience makes their testimony more valid to skeptical researchers. Plus, having more than one surviving experiencer in many of these events has allowed researchers to compare the near-death and shared death experiences for similarities and other qualities. This has already been done in some of the case studies in this book, and the results are chillingly similar. As more case studies are brought together, researchers will be able to take a more methodical approach to this line of investigation.

Rather than try to explain how a phenomenon so great as a shared death experience takes place, I most often like to observe the sense of wonder and serenity on the face of a person who is telling me what it was like to accompany a loved one into a heavenly realm. It is then, when I see the total joy in their face, that I relax about trying to explain these experiences and accept them for the wondrous experiences that they are. In short, I drop my scientific skepticism, quit asking, "Are we there yet?" and just enjoy the view that is provided for me by the people who offer their case studies. They are the ones who truly know when we get there and what we see when we arrive. By all accounts, it is beautiful.

For nearly fifty years I have labored on the cutting edge of near death studies. I have listened to thousands of people tell deeply personal stories about their journey to a world beyond. I have marveled at nearly every aspect of these death experiences, from the sometimes bizarre way in which people almost die to the journey that takes them zooming up a tunnel to meet dead relatives and see their life reviewed one detail at a time.

Each and every shared death and near-death experience is different, yet they all contain similar elements. And when the person who has had one returns to normal consciousness, they are almost always convinced that the body we live in is just a mortal shell, and that our spirit is eternal. "I now know that we live forever," is a common refrain. "I am no longer afraid of death because it's just another plane of existence," is another.

I have heard these comments thousands of times, and I now think that these lucky individuals have taken a brief but significant voyage into the afterlife. The truth is in these voyages. Although there is always something that will stand in the way of scientifically proving life after death, the truth about this subject may just lie with those who have experienced it. I have listened to thousands of people tell their stories of "going to the other side," and I can tell you that I believe what they say, and can tell you that for most of them, nothing stands in the way of their faith that another world awaits them.

"As though I am walking on air"

Shared death experiences carry with them redemption, hope, grace and transformation. Add these elements to the supernatural elements of traveling into a heavenly realm *after* a loved one has died and you have something that is truly impossible for a feeling individual to deny.

This final story contains all the power of a shared death experience and reveals why I consider them a picture window into the afterlife. It was told to me by a woman I'll call June, who introduced her story by telling me what a thoroughly mean man her father was.

"It's true," she said. "Although he never said a cross thing to me or gave me a dirty look, he had so much hatred for everyone else in town that they thought he was insane."

Oddly enough, he was nice to his family and even at times very tender. But if he was out in public or if someone dared to come to their house, June's father would become abusive and protective. June said that the rare visitor would find her father pacing like a guard before them while her poor mother wrung her hands and hoped her husband's anger didn't boil over.

Humiliation was the rule. June said that many times she would hear other kids referring to "that mean old Yankee who lives on Oak Street." At the same time, her mother could never really hold onto a friend because of her husband's erratic ways. She died of a heart attack when June was ten, a death she attributes to the stress caused by her father's "hatred of humanity."

When June was thirty-eight, her father was diagnosed with pancreatic cancer and given a short time to live. In an odd way, said June, the diagnosis was a blessing. I'll let her take over the story:

"All of this might sound tragic but it wasn't. Father's death revealed to me without any reservation that there's an afterlife. I saw my father transform right before my eyes into a gentle and caring man.

"It started two months before he died. I was sitting on the porch and he came out with deep concern on his face. 'June,' he said, 'there is no way I can make it up to all of those people I've hurt over the years. But Brit [June's mother] came to me last night and said she was coming soon to take me away and to make amends before I leave.'"

He had never believed in ghosts or the afterlife, said June, but his change in attitude left no doubt in her mind that some kind of transformation had taken place. The two sat out on the porch until late, talking about the vision he'd had of his wife and what he could do to accomplish her request. The two decided that he should go door to door with his daughter and apologize to everyone he had offended. The next day they set out on that difficult task. For the next three weeks, June and her father made the rounds of everyone he had offended. As they looked at him with puzzlement, June's father told them that he was about to die and offered a heartfelt apology. Some would engage him in long conversations while others accepted his apology and let it go at that. By the end of the three weeks, June's father had accomplished his goal. Now he was tired and ready to die.

It was then, said June, that she shared in an experience that changed her life.

"On the day my father died, he was peaceful and calm. He asked for water, but other than that we sat completely transfixed by a beautiful music that seemed to be just coming out of the air. 'Do you hear that music?' my father said. 'I've never heard anything like that.' Neither had I.

"He lay down on the couch and seemed to almost shut off. Then, to my surprise, it seemed as though a spirit body of him sat up. It was beaming with joy. I heard him say 'good-bye,' and right in front of him stood my mother and aunt. There are no words to describe the appearance of the three of them as spirits. The main thing I can say is that they were all spirit bodies and my mother was looking at me with great joy. And then that was it. The spirit bodies faded away and I was alone with my father's body."

"As you can imagine," said June, "I have never been the same. There was a connection with my mother, my aunt, Dad and God all at once. From that day onward I have felt as though I am walking on air."

June's story left me speechless. Many of them do. Even after all of these years I still wonder, if these aren't proof of life after life, what are they?